W9-AQF-225

THE TOUCH OF GOD

CHARLES R. MEYER

A Theological Analysis
of Religious Experience

THE TOUCH
OF GOD

BTQ 245 .M48 ST. JOSEPH'S UNIVERSITY STX
The touch of God;

3 9353 00007 1322

BR
110
M48

alba house
A DIVISION OF THE SOCIETY OF ST. PAUL
STATEN ISLAND, NEW YORK 10314

125955

Library of Congress Cataloging in Publication Data

Meyer, Charles Robert, 1920-
 The Touch of God.

   Bibliography: p.

   1. Experience (Religion) I. Title

BR110.M48   248.2   75-38978

ISBN: 0-8189-0237X

Nihil Obstat:
   Daniel V. Flynn, J.C.D.
   Censor Librorum

Imprimatur:
   James P. Mahoney
   Vicar General, Archdiocese of New York
   November 2, 1971

   The nihil obstat and imprimatur are official declarations that
   a book or pamphlet is free of doctrinal or moral error. No
   implication is contained therein that those who have granted
   the nihil obstat and imprimatur agree with the contents, opinions
   or statements expressed.

Copyright 1972 by the Society of St. Paul,
2187 Victory Blvd., Staten Island, New York 10314

   Designed, printed and bound in the U.S.A. by the Pauline
   Fathers and Brothers of the Society of St. Paul, 2187 Victory
   Blvd., Staten Island, N. Y. 10314 as part of their communications
   apostolate.

CONTENTS

1

RELIGIOUS EXPERIENCE IN THEOLOGY TODAY

The most important question for theology is and has always been the one about the existence of God. Theologians of the recent past have relied upon rational proofs for God's existence. They have argued that since all experienced being is contingent, God must exist. Logic demands a reason for everything. All things that exist do exist because there is a cause that brought them into being. The ultimate Cause, the uncaused Cause, is God. St. Thomas Aquinas is celebrated in the history of theology for having pointed out five ways of developing this argument for the existence of God from contingency and causality by focussing on inertia, or the need of a mover in any motion; on the impossibility of an infinite series of effecters; on the lack of existential necessity in observable being; on the grades of perfection in creation; on the existence of order in the universe.

There are some theologians today who would question the validity of a proof for the existence of God which proceeds by way of logical argument. If a logical argument is valid, they say, what is had in the conclusion must be in some way implicitly present already in the premises. When such an argument deals with the question of existence, an issue so basic and radical that no fuller noetic grasp of it is possible through analysis or synthesis, through comparison or analogy, its conclusion is only the articulation of a pre-existing judgment. In other words, any logical proof for the existence of God is only a variation of the well-known ontological argument of St. Anselm which has generally been rejected by philosopher and theologian alike.

Other theologians are less radical. They would not reject logical proofs as totally invalid. They might, however, question the relevance of such arguments in today's world. The "now" generation expresses a certain disaffection for tedious metaphysical thought; it manifests on the other hand a mounting interest in the unprovable but experience-related transcendental. Astrology, oriental mysticism, extra-sensory perception, psychedelic trips: these are the intriguing and fascinating preoccupations of a growing number of people today.

The proofs of St. Thomas emanate from a culture that was far more philosophically orientated than ours. The Aristotelian metaphysics upon which they were based was fashioned in a scientific matrix which modern sophistication must reject. Current science has to be believed. It has produced the amazing technology that is part and parcel of the lives of everyone. And modern science is diametrically opposed to the presuppositions of Aristotelian science. For the Stagirite the more inert a being is, the less it is subject to change, the more perfect it has to be. That is why his god is the unmoved mover, the immutable one, who in no way encompasses change within himself. Motion and change are signs of potentiality, of contingency, of corruptibility. No physicist today could accept such a definition of perfection. The totally static being (if one could be conceived of) would be so unproductive as to be deemed hardly a worthy object of scientific research. An absolute zero energy state could hardly be considered the equivalent of perfection achieved. On the contrary, the more mass is converted into energy, the more active a being is, the more fully it is in motion, the more valuable an object for study it becomes for the scientist. He might well consider the perfect being to be that which is total energy, completely in motion. The physicist is caught up in the investigation of myriad particles of varying mass, velocity, magnetic moment, charge and spin. He relentlessly pursues leptons, mesons and baryons. He is in search of a metaphoton for which now at least the theoretical montage has been constructed. It is the tachyon, the particle so highly energized that its velocity exceeds that of the erstwhile absolute c, the speed of light. The computers and theoreticians' drawing boards tell him that the existence of such a particle is now possible—and that within the framework of the Einsteinian formula $E = mc^2$!

The modern world is wary of the classical proofs for the existence of God. It perhaps justly fears that what might emerge from the reasoning processes is not a God that can be in any way squared off with the metaphysical principles enate in current physics, or not a God that it recognizes as the God of Christian revelation, but the god of Aristotle, a pagan god!

The modern world is afraid that the contingency-necessity relationship might well be only a construct of the logical mind, a mind that projects its need for order upon reality. It is too painfully aware of the fruitless search for a verification of the law of parity in nature.

Nor indeed has theology always felt the need for these classical proofs for the existence of God. The Christian faith managed to wax strong for thirteen centuries without them. In the early Church Platonism supplied the philosophical lattice-work upon which theology grew. Its ethos was diametrically opposed to Aristotelianism. The Stagirite's metaphysics attempted to be objective. Ontological principles had to be founded on physical, material reality. In this sense they had to be scientific. But for the Platonists the material world was not the real world at all. It was merely a shadowy reflection and symbol of the real world, the world of ideas. Platonistic metaphysics highlighted the subjective. By means of his mind the human subject was able to participate in the great real world of ideas. The symbolic material world served only to suggest ideas to the thinker.

The Kantian revolution in philosophy tended to reinstate

subjectivist methodology in theology. For the subjectivist the only proof of God that is possible is his experience of "the starry sky above him and the moral law within his breast." To be sure, in Kantianism and the subjectivist philosophies springing from it there is no absolute recrudescence of Platonism. Modern philosophy represents more of a synthesis between the subjectivist and objectivist positions much after the fashion of the Hegelian dialectic. An attempt is made to break down the old dichotomy, so clearly enunciated by Descartes, between the subjective and objective. Reality can be grasped by man only in terms of the meaning he attaches to it. What exists can be apprehended as existent for man only in the reflexive act by which he takes hold of both himself as subject and it as object. What actually is must be significant for someone in order to exist as far as he is concerned. To represent the mind does not, as Aristotle contended, become all things; it remains forever just mind.

Modern philosophy challenges the validity of the assumption upon which Aristotelianism and Scholasticism are based: the objectivity of metaphysical being. Is there really a being that lies beyond the phenomenological universe and the sciences that attempt to categorize and explain it, a being that lies between the physical and purely intentional orders, a real being that is in no way sensible like material things, and still not just a logical construct, like time, or a line or point in geometry? Can being exist really in analogical orders?

Modern thought is reluctant to limit man in his ability to give meaning to reality, to upend it, conquer it and use it. This subjectivist orientation of philosophy may be seen by some as better corresponding with the biblical view of man's noetic capabilities. The author of Genesis sees in Adam's power to name the beasts, to give meaning to what he experiences, the source of his mastery over the universe. And the ecological crisis today has fixed man's attention on his understanding, use and control of his environment. Man is responsible for his understanding of and mastery over the world in which he lives.

Bernard Lonergan in his philosophy of human insight, with a proper nod to data supplied by psychological researchers, opines that human infancy is characterized by a preoccupation with reality over meaning. Meaning for the infant is sought through the medium of contacting reality. But in the adult the process is reversed. The adult seeks to know the world beyond immediate experience. And here reality must be mediated by meaning. If I know that ice is really frozen water, it is because I have attached a certain meaning to the substance I know as water, a meaning which is valid amid varying phenomenological aspects of the substance. For the adult reality is comprehensible only in terms of meaning. Reality is and can be sought only in the matrix of meaning. What has no meaning or no apparent meaning nonplusses the adult. He cannot comprehend it, real though it may be. There is a large sculpture by Picasso in the Chicago Civic Center. Every day hundreds of people pause amid the hustle and bustle of their daily routine to contemplate it. No one can deny its existence. It is big and real enough. But one does not have to be a mind-reader to know the question that is most frequently asked about it. What does it mean? What does it signify?

The Greek world was that of philosophical and theological infancy. The modern world is one come of age. For the ancients what was important was static and fixed reality to be given a meaning. The modern world is more concerned in achieving an ever deepening meaningfulness whereby reality or phenomena can be more closely linked to man. The Greek world limelighted the total achievement that is man, man as object, man so perfect in his masterful attainments, man so mysterious and yet so understandable, man in whose image the gods were made. The world today emphasizes the possibility for transcendence that is man, man as subject, so perfectible, so completely incomprehensible, man made in the image of God.

The indisputable fact is that the God of revelation is not the god of Aristotle. The concept of God that emanates from the classical arguments for his existence is only in a very limited way reconcilable with the description he has given of himself in his word. And if theology has dared in the past so to depart from revelation as to see him as unchanging, apathetically aloof from man's history, unaffected by human weal or woe, indeed, in a totally different order of being, that is only analogous to the one in which man finds himself, it might be rash enough today to allow a serious re-examination of God in biblical terms, terms it has repudiated some time ago by branding them "anthropomorphic."

The search for meaning is, as was said, modern philosophy's attempt to reconcile and synthesize preponderantly subjectivist or objectivist positions in bygone metaphysical and noetic systems. If such a search for meaning in relation to the question of God were limited to a study of the bible and other attestations of an encounter with the divine we would immediately be faced with two problems. The first is what K. Löwith and others have identified as the enigma of the hermeneutic circle. The meaning that is gleaned from a particular event is to a certain extent determined by the question that is asked about it. New questions grow out of the initial understanding, and an unending chain of preconditioned responses is forged. The same difficulty encountered in establishing logical proofs for the existence of God would be found as well in this methodology. The fallacy of *petitio principii*, of already presupposing what is to be established, might be involved in it. At least it would be difficult to distinguish what is valid and what is fallacious in such a procedure. Secondly, any new consideration of past experience would tend to have a relativizing effect upon it. The experiential past simply cannot be recovered in its totality with the precise and full meaning attached to it at the time it occurred. Science today has to admit that the human mind itself is conditioned by man's historical situation. This implies, of course, that in different eras different symbols have to be employed to preserve at least essentially the meanings attached to significant events. In being faithful to the past the interpreter cannot betray the present; otherwise his work would have no significance whatsoever. In translating a past experience into current usage it might prove impossible or extremely difficult to find perfectly corresponding symbol systems.

If a current personal experience of God is made the basis for affirming his existence, the problems that we have considered thus far disappear. Though a reasoning process may be part of an experience, as will be explained later, the validity of the experience itself is not established through such a process. Moreover, one does not readily deny the existence of what one experiences. The existence of God would cease to be a problem for those who have experienced his presence. In this case, however, there is a shift of the problematic from the question of *existence* to the issue of *identity*. I do not deny the existence of what I experience, but how do I know that what I experience is *God,* and not something else?

This is the point at which the biblical data and the interpretation given to them become significant. Although they do not establish the existence of God for me, they can assist me in identifying what I experience as God or not God, provided that I am able to appreciate and translate into my experience the meaning or significance they attach to God.

To be sure, there are other criteria that can assist me in identifying the object of my experience as divine. The first Vatican Council decreed that it is possible for man to come to a certain knowledge of God from the things he experiences in the world. Indeed, this statement did not, as some had hoped it would, vindicate the idea that the existence of God could be proved by logical argument. Nor did it propose that all men actually come to know God in this way. Still less would it want to minimize the necessity of revelation for a more adequate and satisfying knowledge of God. It apparently intends only to point up the fact that man's experience of himself in the world can, apart from any consideration of revelation, encompass the possibility of being aware of and positively identifying God. In his epistle to the Romans (1, 20) St. Paul had also noted such a human capability. Nor does it seem unreasonable that if man has the power to give meaning to his experiences, to classify them and evaluate them, he should also be able at least in some rudimentary way to identify the object or the presence that is involved in them. This basic insight that is the peculiar endowment of human kind is the pivotal point in any theory of knowledge, and to deny it would be to forsake all validity in human cognition. The exact natural criteria that one would use for distinguishing what is divine from what is not would vary from culture to culture, and perhaps even from person to person, but as humanity grows in maturity and consequently in the ability to assign and sort out meaning, these criteria become more definite and secure. Certainly to avoid danger of solipsistic delusion they must be referred to and validated by the experience of others. It is to set forth some of these natural criteria as well as those to be gleaned from revelation that this essay was written.

If, however, this is the case, if my criteria for attributing a divine meaning to my experience have to be compared for validation with those of others, then the problem of the hermeneutic circle might recur. If my interpretation of experience follows in some way from subjective dispositions that in some way or other have been imposed by others, from the way I apprehend myself in relation to them at the time I am analyzing my experience, from the questions they pose for me to ask about it, from the reassurances they give me about it, then should they be strong believers in this sort of thing, I am bound to come to the conclusion that I experienced God. The identity of the object I experience will be determined by the presuppositions of my questions. But is this necessarily true? To the extent that what I have learned previously whether by myself or from others is the matrix in which I have to receive, comprehend, interpret and evaluate every new experience, it is true. But this is the necessary condition of human knowledge. Most of the meanings I attach to reality I have learned from others, from the questions they forced me to ask about objects I encountered, from the criteria they exemplified in their own noetic processes and methodologies and communicated to me. Without such a hermeneutic cycle learning would be impossible. I would not be able to identify anything in a way that would be intelligible to others or hold any meanings in common with them. But to the extent that what I personally have experienced is necessarily prejudged by the hermeneutic criteria they communicate to me to guide me in the interpretation of my own experience, it is not true. Criteria by their very nature are at least bivalent if not polyvalent. They make me the ultimate judge of whether to say yes or no. They are mere guidelines for that judgment. They have to be open to the possibility of at least two if not more interpretations or meanings that can be attached to experience. If they are true criteria in no way can they impose judgment.

It is the plurality of possible meanings inherent in any set of criteria, then, that throws the responsibility for actual judgment of an experience back upon the insight of the subject. He knows the criteria and the possible meanings they hold forth, the identifications they render feasible. He has had the experience. His unique personal insight does for him what no objective norm, or no other person, can. It allows him to judge. He can attach the definite meaning to his experience. He can identify its object. It is this insightful judgment that breaks the hermeneutic circle for any individual deliberating his own experience.

Thus if I say I had an experience of a mysterious presence

that was other-worldly and awesome, and someone tells me that God is other-worldly and awesome, I might at first be inclined to identify my experience as an experience of God. But if it occurs to me that the devil is also other-worldly and awesome, the bivalence of the criteria I was given becomes apparent. So they do not really direct my judgment identifying my experience. If I bring other criteria to bear on the case, they, too, will ultimately be perceived to be bivalent in some way or other, at least to the extent that they would not completely eliminate the possibility that the whole experience might have been purely psychic, an illusion or hallucination, and so will not really decide the issue for me. Ultimately I must use my insight to break the impasse and identify the experience in the light of the criteria given.

From this resolution of a difficulty that might be lodged against the methodology that has been thus far inculcated there emanates a principle that is most fundamental to the development of this essay. In the final analysis it is only the experiencer who can authentically identify his experience. No one else, no set of principles, no guidelines, not even an angel from heaven can make a valid judgment about it. They can only assist in presenting criteria, possible meanings and interpretations, helps and aids to the insight that must eventually intervene and judge.

The great German philosopher Friedrich Nietzsche has encouraged the practice of self-denial in the matter of religious experience. "Our great renunciation," he says, "is not to deify the unknown." Truly a greater renunciation would be to refrain from prejudging the experience of others, to let them be the judges of their own experience.

The second difficulty mentioned above, the problem of historical relativism, might apply to biblical criteria set up for the interpretation of religious or quasi-religious experience. Really though, this issue becomes significant only when there is a question of preserving propositional accuracy from era to era. To preserve the content it sometimes becomes necessary to modify the language. In the realm of experience, however, it is quite another matter. Experience is correlated by a certain empathic insight, and it would seem to make little difference whether contemporaries or people separated from one another by centuries are involved, as long as the experience that is being compared is truly human. A person today can feel as much empathy for the experiences of Cleopatra as for those of his next-door neighbor. The reason that the gospels have remained an object of interest and study down through the centuries is that they have produced so great an empathic insight in the hearts of their readers. The propositional content, save for the scholar, is in a sense, irrelevant, so long as the sentences convey the proper human experience. Thus it may seem an impossible task to translate the symbolic images of scripture into criteria which will jibe perfectly with the understanding of today's science-ridden world. And indeed it might be. But that is not necessary. All that is needed is sufficient adjustment to produce enough correspondence on an experiential level to bring about the kind of empathic insight we have been considering. When such empathy is produced a person will, in the light of biblical and other criteria, be able to identify his experience as truly one of God.

The validity of proceeding to God through experience rather than by logical argument need not be established for the believing Christian. The Christian faith is as a matter of fact founded upon religious experience, not upon logic, science or philosophy. It is a series of acknowledged theophanies that gave rise to the Judaeo-Christian tradition about God. To be a Christian means not only to acknowledge some kind of at least minimal experience of God in one's own life (for one could hardly have an active faith without taking hold of God in some way) but also to affirm rather significant experiences of the divine in the lives of Jesus and those who pioneered the faith with him. It is high time that theology divorce itself from the attractions of an effete philosophy to the extent needed to focus some attention upon the crucial issue of religious experience.

To be sure, this is not a new plea. Voices have raised this cry in the past. Most notable among the recent advocates of a more holistic approach to the question of the divine in human life is Rudolf Otto. His *Idea of the Holy* aroused the interest of many, but until very recently has had little significant influence on Roman Catholic theology.

Otto is fascinated by the uncanny. He decries the fact that the fear or dread of God is no longer felt. It is for this reason that in a sense God can be said to be dead. The rational element in theology, in religious discourse, and indeed in rendering the scriptures themselves predominates and stifles whatever else might be aroused in the human heart. The idea of the holy is peculiarly applicable to the religious sphere. It conveys the notion that other-worldly reality is inexpressible and indeed not fully conceivable. But in today's world even this word has lost its impact in religious life. The uncanniness of the holy is no longer felt. The word is most frequently applied in the ethical sphere where it becomes a factor in a kind of calculus of virtues. The one who is holy is one who is completely passive; the one who does nothing exciting.

Schleiermacher made an attempt to rouse a "creature-consciousness" that might have restored emotional contact with the numinosity of the divine. But the setting in which his endeavor was cast was one of philosophical analysis.

Religious groups, however, still retained the wherewithal of religious experience. Exercises of piety, participation in mystical rites and liturgies, the aura that surrounds ancient ecclesial buildings and monuments, contact with the numinous past established by readings and sermons; all tended to engender a sense of the presence of some kind of *mysterium tremendum*.

The Old Testament is full of evidence for the fact that the experienced presence of Yahweh could have a paralyzing effect upon man. Before him even the heavenly hosts could only stand in awe and proclaim his ineffable numinosity in the chant: "Holy, holy, holy!"

For Otto as for Recejac all mystical experience has to begin with a feeling of fear and terror. He agrees with James that the element of mystery is paramount in inculcating a sense of presence for that which is not seen: "The darkness held a presence that was all the more felt because it was not seen."

The New Testament also dwells upon God's power. Even the word St. Paul often employs for grace signifies power: God's own power given to man. More recent theology often interpreted grace in an entirely passive way: it is seen as a purely static endowment of the human soul rendering it pleasing to God. But early Christianity understood grace as a divine energy leading man to orgy, to a burst of divinely directed activity.

While the emphasis of more recent theology has been on establishing some kind of viable concept of God, the ancient Church understood full well (from writers like St. Augustine) that if one has constructed an unassailable concept of God, one thing is certain: what has been conceived is not God.

For Otto the fascination of the mysterious, of the wholly other, like the fascination of sex, springs from man's ineluctable desire to know, to penetrate the secret, to master the indomitable. The numinous fills man with not only a sense of bewilderment and confusion, but also with a strange exhilaration, a feeling of ravishment that captivates and transports him at times to a state of dizzy intoxication. Here is the Dionysian element in religious experience.

Otto sees the writings of some of the great mystics of the past permeated with this Dionysian spirit and élan. He cites as an example the poem of St. Bernard entitled *Urbs Sion*. One must stand in awe of its deeply mystical thrust. It is eminently eschatological, numinal, graphic, concrete, emotional.

According to Otto, many reject the mystical way because the rational approach to God is less threatening, less demanding, "cooler" as a medium. The ordinary Christian, perhaps because of a false humility, has to say: "This is not for me." So the only grasp he will have on God will be with his intellect, if indeed he can in any way comprehend the *via causalitatis, eminentiae et negationis!*

Then too it is easier for the preacher to inculcate his message with simple rational arguments. There really can be no direct transmission of religious feeling in the proper sense. It cannot be taught. It can only be awakened in man's spirit by God's Spirit. Words can only set the scene for it to occur; they can in no sense cause it.

In Otto's estimation one of the greatest contributions of Martin Luther to religion is the notion that if a person does not himself feel and experience the numinal, then no preaching, singing or telling of it can help him.

The preoccupation of ancient writers with miracles is hardly accidental. Miraculous occurrences can directly engender the eerie feeling of the numinous. By virtue of what they are, they establish contact with the uncanny. Thus Schiller terms the miracle the dearest child of faith.

Religious feeling, so necessary to the Christian life, has been diminished by a number of historical contingencies. Strangely enough, the Incarnation itself, according to Otto, to the extent that it made God, the one who is really wholly Other, more easily translatable in human terms, hurt the sense of awe from which true religious experience emanates. Many of the Fathers of the Church succumbed to anthropomorphizing descriptions of the divine, some to the extent of falling into heresy.

But especially the incursion of Platonist and Stoic philosophical formulas into early Christian theology has done irreparable harm to religion. For these philosophies presented apathy as the central characteristic of divinity. And since the pursuit of perfection inculcated in the gospels demanded that

God in as much as it is possible be emulated by man, passivity became the ideal of the Christian life. Some of the Latin Fathers like Lactantius fought against this idea. They resented the representation of God as a "Big Daddy" or "Goodygoody." A god who is conceived of as having no passions, as being totally untouchable, would indeed be the god of the Stoics, but not the living God evisaged by scripture.

Disputes among medieval theologians of intellectualist and voluntarist persuasions tended to play down the power and majesty even of the divine will. Since the intellectualist party under the aegis of St. Thomas eventually won out, a modifiable will in God came to be regarded as dangerous a concept as that of divine passions. God was pictured as a massive Intellect, and the ideal of the Christian life came to be centered in a faith-assent to propositions, rather than in charitable action or compassion. It was the Lutheran concept of faith that ultimately challenged this view and attempted to restore religious feeling to its rightful place in the Christian life.

These penetrating analyses of Rudolf Otto simply cannot be cast aside in a world whose chief theological thrust is in the direction of ecumenism. It is eminently clear that what is being called for is a re-examination of the foundations of the Christian faith in scripture, experience and the authentic traditions of the people of God in the hope of constructing a more complete and meaningful theology that will take into account the alogical structures of human life. Only when religious experience is taken as the starting point as well as the guiding star of such an investigation will this feat become possible. It is the purpose of this essay to supply some initial reflection on the topic of religious experience which might be helpful in the monumental task of retooling Catholic theology to cope with this challenge. There is hardly a fuller larder of religious symbols than in Catholicism; yet there is scarcely a theology that is as undernourished in the area of experience and sentience.

We have said that the faith which we hold in common and confess as a people is founded on a religious experience engendered by a theophany we call Christ. But it is reasonable to assume also that the faith of each individual must be founded, if not, to be sure, on a theophany, at least on a theopathy or experience of the divine. For faith can come only through grace. And grace is the extension of God's loving presence into the life of an individual.

There are many questions that can be posed about grace. Is it supernatural? Is it a created being or God himself? In what sense is it divine, and in what sense human, etc.? It is not my intention in this essay to answer these questions. I have treated them in a previous work entitled *A Contemporary Theology of Grace,* and to go into them again here would deter us from our main objective, a discussion of religious experience. This is not to say that the two issues are not most intimately connected. They most certainly are. But to consider religious experience as a grace, to consider it from the standpoint of God, as it were, belongs to the scope of my other work, not to this one.

But certainly this question can be legitimately asked here. An experience is something that I can sense and feel; can the presence of God to which I respond in faith be sensed and felt? If grace is to be termed supernatural (whether it really is or not is a question considered in my former work) can I have an experience of it?

Many people would admit the possibility of sensing the presence of God in the case of the saints and mystics, but would eschew any consideration of it in their own case. Actually, they would say, they have never sensed it. Of them the further question might be asked: would they recognize it if they did experience it? Would they be able to identify it as an experience of God? Some Catholics, because of their misunderstanding of the theology of grace, have never allowed for themselves even the possibility of experiencing God's presence, and consequently they can say they never did feel the operation of grace in their lives.

The Council of Trent (Sixth session, chapter 9 and canon 13) proposed the notion that no one can know with the certitude of faith that his sins have been remitted, and that he has consequently been promoted to a state of grace. Theologians have extended this teaching to encompass any kind of rigorous and strict certitude. They allow only what St. Thomas calls a "conjectural certitude," that is, one based upon the fact that a person observes the commandments for a considerable length of time, is devoted to prayer, flees from worldly amusements, loves to be occupied with spiritual things, and the like. The later scholastics admitted that a person could have moral certitude about the fact that he was in the state of grace, that is, a certitude that excludes the probability, but not the absolute possibility, of error.

Now it is possible to see how the question of certitude can be very easily confused with the question of experience. It might seem obvious that one should be able to be sure about what one experiences, so that if one were to have an experience of grace, he could know for certain that he was in the state of grace. But clearly there are a number of fallacies in this line of argumentation. First of all, the theologians' case is about the state of grace. This is to be considered as a perduring condition. What is said is that one cannot be certain about a perduring condition of grace. But an experience is a passing situation of man. Thus one might well be certain about an experience of grace, but entertain some doubt about whether he is in the state of grace. In other words, he might be aware of the fact that he had an actual grace, but not certain whether it brought him to the state of mind required for the acquisition of habitual grace. Secondly, certitude refers to the tenacity of assent that is made to a proposition (the one in the case being: "I am in the state of grace"), but an experience is prior to all propositions. If an experience of God is to be reduced to a proposition it would be: "I have had an experience of God," not "I am in the state of grace." Obviously for the second proposition more data would be required. Thirdly, it is possible even to have an experience without being certain about what kind of an experience it is. Not all that is experienced is as certain as may some time appear.

Perhaps the source of the confusion in the minds of many about certitude concerning the state of grace and an experience of grace is to be found in a brief argument of St. Thomas (S.T. 1, 2, q. 112, a. 5); it runs in this fashion: "It is not possible to have certitude about anything unless one can be sure about its cause. The cause of the state of grace, however, is God inasmuch as he is the author of grace. But as the author of grace he cannot be known by natural reason. Therefore one cannot be sure about the state of grace." Here St. Thomas seems to be saying that God, precisely as imparting grace, cannot be perceived by natural reason. Once again it would seem that a distinction has to be made between an experience and reasoning about the data in the experience. I experience color. I am certain of this. But I cannot be certain about the cause of color. I cannot be sure whether the color I experience is formally in the object or in an electro-chemical reaction of the cones in the retina of my eye. In other words, St. Thomas does not seem to want to deny the possibility of having an experience of God. Certainly the prophets must have had such an experience (cf. S.T. 3, q. 30, a. 3, ad 1). What he states is that without a special revelation it is not possible to know that an experience of God's presence implies precisely the bestowal of grace, that is, of sanctifying grace. Even sinners can prophesy. The experience of God in a prophetic vision is a *gratia gratis data*. So an experience of God does not necessarily impart certitude about the fact that one is in the state of sanctifying grace, that one enjoys the *gratia gratum faciens* (cf. also *Super Evangelium S. Ioannis Lectura*, n. 1578).

Thus the Council of Trent acknowledges the possibility

that one can through a special revelation know for certain even that he is among the predestined (Session 6, chapter 12). So too theologians do not deny the possibility of this kind of revelatory experience of God, though they do not consider it to be common.

In spite of the persuasion to the contrary in the minds of many, traditional theology, then, does not preclude the possibility of the actual experience in some way of grace or of the presence of God. Nor is this possibility restricted, at least in the teaching of one school of theology, to the case of certain special people like mystics and saints. Theologians like Sandreau, Lamballe, Louismet, Garrigou-Lagrange, Joret and Arintero stress the idea that all are called to perfection, and the ordinary way to it is through infused contemplation, which implies, to say the least, some real, if general and not well-defined, experiential perception of God's presence.

In his essay "Natur und Gnade" Karl Rahner excoriates the idea of a "state" of grace that is "present," but not active to the extent that it can in some way be perceived, as an aberration from the biblical doctrine about grace. He points out the desire of modern man to experience grace, to feel its power at work in daily life. He emphasizes the importance in current theology of the idea of uncreated grace, that is, of the special presence of God himself to the justified person. Grace primarily is God himself communicated to man in loving kindness. This presence must make some difference in the conscious life of the one who enjoys it. Scripture employs such terms as "life," "comfort," "anointing," "light," etc., to designate grace, and all of these signify radically experiential realities. One school of theology describes actual graces formally as "enlightenments" and "inspirations"; again there is a clear reference to psychic movements that can be felt. Implicit in this Molinist school's adherence to these terms is the desire to express the fact that every supernatural act differs from its purely natural counterpart not only ontologically or entitatively, but also consciously and existentially.

This awareness of grace does not necessarily signify that grace can be identified as a directly experienced object of the mind. Rather the issue seems to revolve about an a-priori condition of human cognition. In every act I am aware of myself not precisely as the object of the act, but rather as the knower, the doer, etc. This awareness is a pre-conceptual given of human consciousness. Similarly in any act I can be pre-conceptually conscious of other modifications of my subjective existence without having to make them the direct objects of my intention. Very often they cannot be fully focussed and identified in a subsequent reflexive act, although they were definitely a conscious part of my initial experience.

Rahner insists upon the idea that there is no real distinction in the present order between what might be termed "pure nature" and "elevated nature." The only real and existential order is one of elevated nature. In perceiving my "natural" acts, if I am graced, I simultaneously but pre-conceptually perceive acts which are elevated.

It is this notion, then, which is being accepted by an increasing number of theologians, that makes possible the investigation that we shall initiate in this essay. The basic question that we shall ask is whether it is possible reflexively to identify the divine elements in our experience, what criteria are to be used in establishing their identity, and what effect they have upon our lives, or should have upon our lives. If indeed it is possible to identify God in an experience, then the problem of the validity of the rational proofs for the existence of God ceases to be the important one for current theology. In fact, the issue of an experienced God may demand the construction of an entirely new theology radically different from the traditional one which proceeded largely by way of rational analysis.

The question of the experience of God is one that is even more vital to ministry than it is to theology. If more than ever before priests and ministers are asking hard questions about their roles, if there is doubt and confusion about what the minister of God should do in today's world when the structures of the past are becoming disjointed and the future is dark and uncertain, one thing has to remain quite evident. It is the task of the minister to point to grace and its sources in the lives of his people. And to do this maybe the minister also has to be aware of the sources of grace in his own life. If he has not the criteria to identify the action of God in either his own or the lives of his people, it is no wonder that he finds his work frustrating, unproductive and dissatisfying. If the people whom he serves find that he cannot help them identify and foster religious elements in their experience, they are not going to give him the kind of support he needs for doing the difficult job he has undertaken. Recent surveys of priests show that the chief source of difficulty in their ministry stems from the fact that their work seems to make no difference to people. It may be that this perceived feedback contains some element of truth. Though they feel that they are doing their pastoral duty in regard to the people, and thus to a certain extent serve also their own needs, many ministers of God are not really meeting the actual needs of the people they think they serve. This may be true because what many people today are looking for from their ministers are not cliches, words of comfort or encouragement, counselling, psychotherapy; maybe they are no longer seeking even sacramental ministrations the way they used to. Maybe what they want above everything else is some kind of experience of the divine. And they look to their ministers to point out the way for them.

2

EXPERIENCE

Before we can proceed to an analysis of religious experience it is necessary to come to some understanding of what we mean by experience itself. From what has already been said, the reader will gather that just as conceptualization is prior and basic to judgment, so experience is an a-priori given and fundament of conceptualization. The first thing we understand about experience is that it is so elemental to life itself that it cannot be fully described or defined. Just as one can come to know what life is only by living, so one can come to know what experience is only by experiencing. Just as we cannot communicate to others fully, accurately and effectively what our life is, so it is impossible to adequately pass on the full meaning of our experience. It is, however, possible to make some observations about it that will deepen our awareness of it, and better delineate its significance in our lives.

The first obvious fact about experience is that it is highly personal. Each experience is unique and unrepeatable. It may seem possible to relive an experience, but this reliving of it is actually a new experience that in some way highlights the essential elements of the previous one. Indeed, an experience cannot be fully recaptured even in an immediately subsequent reflection upon it. Only certain aspects of it can be focussed by attention; many of the data originally experienced will be lost forever. The significant elements in an experience, however, can be fixed in the memory, and can leave their mark permanently in the psyche of the subject.

An experience is simple and basic enough to defy description, and at the same time complex enough to preclude the possibility of full conceptualization. For in an experience thousands of bits of information at various levels of consciousness are fed into the psyche. Experiences are the building blocks of all conceptualizations; yet even over a lifetime an individual will not find it possible to form concepts covering all of the data supplied in a single rich experience. The conscious part of the psyche can only scan those elements of an experience that have sufficient stimulational force as to make them worthy of note, while bits of an experience that lack significance or relevance to the mood and condition of the subject are passed over and perhaps lost forever.

When we come to consider how experience is to be correlated with consciousness, we have to be alert to avoid the error of seeing experience simply as the result of conscious activity. In reality experience is a wider concept than that of consciousness. For an experience is the result of the operation of both positive and negative consciousness. It comprises an awareness of both the extent and limitations of consciousness. To be sure, an experience has to be founded primarily on consciousness. Where there is no consciousness, there can be no experience. But conscious aspects are really only a part of an experience. Sleep is certainly an experience; yet in it consciousness is greatly reduced. In a deep coma, there may be very little evidence of any kind of consciousness at all. Yet the person aroused from such a coma will be sure that he has had an experience. It would have largely to be described as an experience of negative consciousness. Indeed, it may be that the fact of a total lack of experience, of non-experience, in a particular area of organic or psychic function could be appropriately described as an experience. People who are blind from birth and have no perception of light at all might be said to have an experience of total blindness. Any experience has to incorporate within itself an awareness or consciousness of some stimulus, as well as a grasp of the non-conscious, that is of the limits of consciousness, of the limen or threshold of consciousness. In some experience that limen is perceived as being, as it were, quite close. This is the case in experiencing a light sleep, where one is not just quite awake. In other experiences that limen seems rather remote, as in the case of being involved in the exciting and tense action of a football game.

It is extremely important for our development later of a theological methodology to cope with religious experience that this notion, which sets forth a definite correlation between experience, positive and negative consciousness, and the limen that separates them, be fully understood.

It is not fully possible to develop a description of experience in terms of negative consciousness, because our thinking tends to be mostly positive. So for practical purposes we think of our experience as resulting from conscious effort, though actually at times the more significant part of it may be the result of negative consciousness.

At this point someone may wonder whether we are resurrecting the old theory of Sigmund Freud about the influence of the unconscious on conscious behavior. We will be reminded that all psychologists today do not look with favor upon this theory, and that many have positively rejected it.

Once again we have to point out that we are not discussing behavior, or the election from which it springs, or the judgment which precedes election or the conceptualizations which are the forerunners of judgment. We are addressing ourselves to something that is much more elemental than all these; we are concerned with experience. Whether what is totally unconscious can influence behavior or not is a question we will leave for the Freudians and anti-Freudians to battle about. All we are trying to state is that what is perceived as not being within the scope of positive consciousness, that is, the negatively conscious, can at times be apprehended as a significant part of an experience.

When we come to consider the question of consciousness

itself, we immediately note four characteristics of it: that it is the foundation of psychic unity; that it has a definite field or scope; that it admits of degrees; and that it tends to transcend itself.

The human organism is a marvelous congeries of highly diversified systems, movements and responses. It is a hotbed of disparate and sometimes antithetical nervous stimuli. The body is constantly subject to catabolic forces which tend to break it down, and anabolic movements which restore and rebuild it. In successive periods of time, it in no sense retains a fully integral identity. In the midst of all of this, consciousness is perceived as the chief unifying factor. It gives rise to the ego, to which each and every one of myriad actions and reactions of the organism as well as its multiple parts is attributed. It gives rise to the concept of the I as the center and director of the whole operation.

Not only the attention, but the scope of awareness of the human organism, is very definitely limited by intrapsychic as well as outside factors. This makes possible an organization and direction of subjective forces by the higher mental and volitional faculties. The human brain contains not only countless synapses or connective devices which permit certain unidirectional chain reactions between different storage and motor areas, but also a large number of inhibitory cells, which prevent random couplings or unwanted sensations. The ego is directly aware not only of what it wants to know, but of the fact that it can shut out or minimize what it does not want to experience. Moreover, in every act of awareness, there is not only a direct comprehension of both the conscious self and the object of which it is conscious, but also of the limits of the field of consciousness. Consciousness is in large measure aptly compared to a field of vision in which certain objects are better focussed than others, and which has a definite horizon or limen beyond which one is not able to see. It might well be likened to a picture of the moon taken from space. In the area lighted by the sun, it is possible to discern various familiar Cynthian landmarks and configurations; in the dark part nothing is clear; between the light and dark sections is what astronomers call the terminator, or line of demarcation. We shall have much more to say about the terminator of consciousness both here and later in connection with religious experience. Here we shall consider it specifically from a psychological standpoint.

The field of consciousness can be extensive and expansive, or it can be narrow and confined. The size of the field is determined by the position of the limen or terminator. All the factors involved in determination of the scope of the field can be a part of an experience. Our knowledge of the dark area in the field of consciousness, or if you will, of negative consciousness and of its influence on experience has been greatly enhanced by studies of hypnosis. Under ideal conditions in some subjects it is possible to limit consciousness in selective areas of the perceptual field, or generally, so that major surgical operations can be performed without anesthesia and with no discomfiture at all. Hypnosis seems to be a condition resulting from a partial repositioning of the terminator of consciousness; it is on the order of that which occurs during sleep, though not as full and extensive in all areas of the conscious field. Some authors have described the hypnotic state as one of negative delusion, that is, as a distortion of perceived reality due to the gaps created in it. It would seem that the terminator of consciousness plays the important role in creating the gaps in perception. The phenomenon that is most astounding about the hypnotic state is a feat that is termed post-hypnotic suggestion. In the hypnotized condition a subject is told that when he wakes up he will not remember what happened to him, but he will perform some particular act, often one that he is not accustomed to. Upon awakening, he will experience a strong urge to follow out the suggestion, though he has absolutely no recollection of why he wants to do this particular thing. The idea of post-hypnotic suggestion shows, it would seem, some stimulational receptiveness even in the dark area of consciousness, and the potential that this area has not only of creating experience, but, at least in this instance, even of influencing behavior. The issues of extrasensory and subliminal perception, like hypnotism, pertain to this dark area of consciousness beyond the terminator.

Within the illuminated area of consciousness psychologists often identify three degrees of concentration. In the focal region are those objects in relation to which the subject is completely alert. They are the brightest objects that appear in his awareness. Beyond this region lies that of peripheral consciousness. Here there is sufficient awareness to permit an experienced object to be completely and accurately recalled, and fully focalized in reflection even though it was not in the center of attention in the original perception. In the outer ranges of the lighted area lies the subconscious, where there is a dim awareness of something that can be recalled by the subject, but not completely identified even in reflection. Beyond the terminator, then, lies what we have called the darkened area of the consciousness. Here there is no direct awareness and no capability of recall on the part of the subject. But, as we explained in the case of post-hypnotic suggestion, here there is some openness and receptivity of the ego to stimuli; here there is a capability for some minimal kind of experience which at times can be recalled through the agency of some power outside of the subject.

What has been said concerning the field and degrees of consciousness cannot, of course, be fully established on scientific grounds. Consciousness cannot be measured quantitatively; consciousness cannot be gauged or calibrated. It cannot even be accurately located. Goltz removed the brain of a dog, which, even without its brain, continued to live for some months and to respond to tactile, audio and visual stimuli, and otherwise give indications of some kind of consciousness. The sole authentic source we have for data about consciousness is our own reflective consciousness.

The limitation of its field as well as the possibility of a

unified succession of different types of fields are conditions that give rise to the tendency of consciousness to transcend itself. There is innate in every individual a thrust to extend the limits of his consciousness. Where this thrust is lacking, where there is no urge to explore, to learn, to concentrate attention, a psychopathic situation is most certainly encountered. The capabilities that some people have of pushing back the terminator in certain areas of consciousness have been always considered mysterious and intriguing. The mind reader, the clairvoyant, the dowser and the autohypnotist have been the subjects of much psycho-physical research. They are regarded by some as exceptional cases of transcendent consciousness. But more ordinary phenomena are well within the experience of almost everyone. We shall consider some of these cases in the following chapter.

Recent research has demonstrated the need of the conscious self for continuous perceptual stimulation. Consciousness must continually transcend itself in experience after experience; stimulus-starvation results in disorientation, disorganization and eventual full loss of unity.

A number of universities have undertaken a psychological study of brainwashing techniques. A student volunteer is placed in a small room. Its walls, ceiling and floor are painted a dull white. He is supplied with diffused light and air, and nothing else. His reactions are noted by observers, and collected by various kinds of sensing devices. He is also asked to report them orally as best he can. He is able to get along fairly well for a few hours, thinking, humming, singing and whistling to himself, and amusing himself with calesthenics. But eventually he becomes hallucinated. He takes a trip quite similar to those which are drug-induced. As his behavior verges on the psychotic, he is removed from the chamber and restored to normal life by the simple process of allowing him to experience ordinary sense-stimuli.

The tendency of consciousness to transcend itself through experience is so strong as to evoke from the imagination and memory random material when no stimulation is provided from the outer senses. The function of inhibitor cells in the brain is apparently impaired, and there bursts into conscious focus a wild assortment of disconnected and grossly distorted material from various storage areas in the cortex. Control of the flow of this material is eventually completely lost, and the consciousness is glutted with a hodge-podge of endogenic sensation. The brain of the subject has indeed been washed.

A similar breakdown of inhibitor cells possibly occurs on a minor scale when a person is unaccountably obsessed or haunted by a tune, the image of a face, a fear, etc.

Conversely, brainwashing may also occur, as more recent studies show, when the sensorium is glutted with external stimulation. After the excitation is removed, the individual's consciousness is expanded, so that he will experience an unusual flow of sensory data just as if he had taken a psychedelic drug.

Some psychologists today are interested in the relationship of both sense starvation and overstimulation to religious phenomena. Were some of the extraordinary religious experiences associated with the lives of the mystics connected with the fact that they were preoccupied with mortifying the senses? Was the bleakness of the desert, or of the monastic cell, a factor in what these saints experienced? What did their fasts and the long hours they spent in motionless meditation have to do with their visions? Can electronic or pharmacological stimulation of the sensorium today produce true religious experience?

Ordinarily consciousness is supplied with data from a set of outer objective stimuli emanating from the sense organs, and a set of inner subjective stimuli originating in the memory, imagination, emotions, mind and will. The various stimulations are held in correct balance and proper interrelation by the activation of certain groups of synapses, connective fibers and inhibitory cells.

The operation of the traditional five senses is well known,

and need not be dwelt upon at any length. However, a word about their limitations and limina might be appropriate to help us understand more about the terminator of consciousness in specific areas of sensation and its effect upon experience.

The two basic characteristics of visual sensation are brightness and color. The human visual apparatus is capable of distinguishing about 600 intensities of brightness ranging from blinding white to jet black. Black is apprehended by the sighted person as a negative experience of light. It is important to note that, though negative, it is a definite visual experience. A person blind from birth reports that he has no more experience of black than he has of white or gray. Once again there is evidence for a dark area of consciousness that is perceived as the foundation of a true experience.

In color vision there is no consciousness of component color frequencies. If two sounds are heard simultaneously, the sum and difference frequencies, the harmonics within range, as well as the distinct fundamentals can be heard. In other words, the ear is able to analyze sounds; but the eye is not able to analyze colors. It is not able to break down mixed hues into fundamental components. Orange is not perceived as a mixture of red and yellow; it is seen as a distinctive and unique color on a par with red and yellow. Mixing, then, is a phenomenon that lies beyond the terminator of visual consciousness.

It takes a certain amount of time for a visual image on the retina to reach the occipital area of the brain and appear in consciousness. An image must remain on the retina for at least 1/10th of a second if it is to be perceived at all, and for at least about 1/5th of a second if its color is to be observed. Visual after-images will be produced by viewing objects of high light intensity and contrast. Very brief exposure will generally produce positive after-images, while longer viewing will result in negative ones. Colored objects will produce varying kinds of after-images according to the laws of color mixture. An adaptive time lag is experienced in moving from highly lighted areas to relatively dark ones, and temporary night-blindness results.

The stroboscopic effect is one of the significant products of the extension or retraction of the terminator of consciousness in visual perceptions. Alternate pulses of high intensity light against a relatively dark background result in interesting perceptions and psychological effects. If you use a strobe light of the proper frequency with a card on which a circular pattern of black lines is printed, and place the card on the turntable of your phonograph, and if your phonograph is moving at the proper speed, there will be no perception of motion at all; you will see each line clearly and distinctly, as if the card were on your desk rather than on a moving turntable. The motion will be beyond the terminator of your visual perception. Similarly, a strobe light on a dance floor will tend to freeze motion; one will have the impression of a continuous series of still tableaux. Still another, seemingly opposite, effect can be produced. The wind direction arrows on a TV weather map seem to be in motion. But your experience tells you that they really are not. They are merely cards on which have been printed striated patterns. The strobe light again gives the impression of motion where really there is none. Max Wertheimer's phi phenomenon produces an impression of color of varying hue as a black and white card is rotated at different speeds, even in ordinary light.

It is possible with a flickering strobe light to induce certain psychological moods or impressions. A person may feel uncomfortable and eventually become hallucinated if exposed for any length of time to a strobe light operating at the rate of about eight flashes per second. Here is another instrument of the brainwashers.

In all of these examples one perceives a definite relationship between the recorded experience and the terminator of consciousness. What lies beyond the terminator somehow affects the experience itself.

There are evidences also of various zones of color vision within the retina of the eye, each with its more or less clearly defined terminator. If the left eye is closed and a small purple object is moved slowly from left to right across the field of vision of the open eye, an experience of changing hue will be produced. At first, the object will appear black, then bluish, violet and finally, in the central field, it will be perceived as purple.

Visual impressions also tend to change in relation to background. For instance, a gray card will seem to be grayer if it is placed upon a pure white card.

The limina of hearing are encountered in the area of intensity, pitch, duration and fatigue. Certain sounds are too weak to be perceived by the human ear, but can be detected with electronic instruments. The upper threshold of pitch for the average adult occurs at a frequency of about 20,000 cycles per second, while the lower auditory vestibule lies in the range of 15 cycles per second. As is the case with the eye, auditory sensations too require a certain time to traverse the proper nerve fibers and reach the appropriate area of the brain. Extremely short pulses of sound will not be perceived because they are below the threshold of duration. The hearing mechanism can become fatigued if subjected to the same tones for long periods of time. Extremely loud sounds seem to diminish in intensity with relation to time of exposure; this seems to be a clear indication that the limen of acuity is changed, particularly when a much weaker sound of a notably different frequency is perceived to be equal in intensity with the stronger one to which the ear has become accustomed. There is also evidence of audio masking in the fact that a tone of one frequency will seem louder when heard alone than when heard at equal intensity with one of another frequency.

One of the peculiar experiential phenomena of sound is the characteristic of dissonance. Some combinations of sound are perceived to be harmonious and pleasing while others are interpreted as strident and dissonant. As far as the input

wave-forms are concerned, there seems to be no special physical difference other than frequency between harmonious and
dissonant tones; the impression created is a construct of the
hearing mechanism or the interpreting consciousness. Here
again one encounters evidence of the operation of a terminator
between pleasant and unpleasant sound in the consciousness,
and this terminator may, to a certain extent, be a product of
cultural experience, since some peoples like the Chinese find
certain tonal combinations pleasing, while western listeners
consider them to be dissonant.

The limina of taste sensations partially overlap with
those of smell. Psychologists usually distinguish four different
fundamental taste experiences: sweetness, sourness, bitterness
and saltiness. It is possible to produce these not only by external stimulation with food, but also internally by injecting
certain substances into the bloodstream. There is a very
definite after-image, as is quite obvious, in taste sensations,
and the limina of duration vary not only in accordance with
the substance tasted, but also in relation to certain subjective
conditions. Taste contrast is another phenomenon of consciousness worth noting. If a substance is sweetened slightly
so that its sweetness is just below the threshold of sensation,
and it is applied to one side of the tongue, it will be immediately perceived as definitely sweet if a salty substance is
brought into contact with the other side of the tongue.

As with the sense of taste, olfactory sensations can also
be aroused with naturally inadequate stimuli, as for instance,
an electric current. Blending of odors has the effect of changing the threshold of perception, and the sense of smell is
well known to have an extremely short limen of duration.
Pungent odors will disappear from consciousness within a
relatively short period of time. Adaptation time depends
largely upon the kind of odor experienced, the concentration
of the stimuli on the end organs of the sense, and various
subjective conditions.

When we come to consider the set of sensations traditionally considered to be tactile, we run into a major difficulty of classification. For through the sense of touch we receive information concerning hardness, wetness, temperature, smoothness, pressure, motion, tickling, irritation, hunger, thirst, nausea, fatigue, pain, sexual pleasure, vibration, various visceral and vesicular conditions, etc. Each one has its own limina which can be narrowed or widened by sensations in another tactile area, as well as by attention, concentration, and a host of other factors. To account for some of these interactions some researchers have postulated the existence of a "common sense." One of the characteristics of tactile sensations is that they generally can be localized. However, the issue of an extended terminator of consciousness in touch sensations poses some very interesting questions. One need only to consider the case of a "phantom limb" in an amputee, or of referred pain in certain visceral disturbances.

The terminator of consciousness plays an important role also in perception. Perception is usually defined as a sense representation resulting from the association or combination of a number of sensations or sense impressions. The sight of a steak in the frying pan, the sizzling sound it makes, the appetizing odor it emits while it is being cooked, the visceral report of an empty stomach: all these sensations combine to form a perception of hunger.

The terminator of consciousness can often extend itself to create perceptual illusions. Our kinesthetic sense, the perception of the relationship of various parts of the body to one another, and to external objects, as well as any change in that relationship, can easily be led astray. If we touch a marble with our index and third finger, we definitely perceive it as a single object. If, however, these fingers are crossed while touching the marble, it will seem that we are in contact with two separate objects. Our static sense gives us an awareness of our position in space. If we spin around for a while in one direction, when we stop, we will have a definite impression of moving in the opposite direction. In the weightlessness of space, it is difficult to distinguish up from down. The perception of external motion is very difficult in certain circumstances. If in a darkened room one light is fixed and another is moved, a viewer will have difficulty in identifying the moving light; some may perceive both lights as being in motion. One's judgment of the speed of a moving body, and even of its direction of motion, is upset if he is placed on a randomly moving platform. The perception of the passage of time is influenced by many psychological factors. Time seems to drag when one is waiting for an important announcement. It seems to fly when one is engaged in some pleasurable occupation. Bi- and tridimensional spatial perception is filled with anomalies. Depth perception is easily thrown awry. No fully satisfying explanation has been given for a number of ordinary phenomena. If one takes his stand at a definite distance from a tall building, and from there observes a man standing two hundred feet away and then approaching to within twenty feet, the image of the man on the retina of the eye will be much larger at the shorter distance; he may even loom larger than the building. Yet the observer will perceive him as being the same size no matter where he stands. At times the moon when perceived on the horizon will seem gigantic. When the same moon is in the zenith, it will appear to be much smaller.

These perceptual experiences can contain data which appear in the consciousness for which no ascertainable external, physical cause can be found. Or, conversely, they can filter out significant data so that they in no way appear in consciousness.

The inner subjective stimuli of consciousness are provided by the imagination, mind, memory, emotions and will.

Imagination is described by some psychologists as the second state of consciousness. It involves a retention, reproduction in whole or part, and sometimes a mixing of sense perceptions. In an exercise of the imagination one can experience a simple, matter-of-fact recall of a particular sense-image, or a series of sensations, or, on the other hand, a truly creative combination of elements or segments of various sense information to produce a perception that is entirely new. In experiencing the working of one's imagination, very often there is an awareness of an even more positive engagement of the psychic forces than is experienced in ordinary sensation. The terminator of consciousness seems, as it were, to be pushed back by positive subjective effort to pave the way for the appearance of a desired, creative image. In other states of the consciousness, however, images of all sorts randomly pop into the conscious field without direction or great expenditure of psychic energy. Sometimes a person cannot rid his consciousness of a haunting melody or a harrowing experience.

Apart from these particular cases, however, in general the field of consciousness is apprehended as narrower in the experience of images than it is in the perception of similar sensations. The terminator of consciousness seems, as it were, to be positioned closer to the subject. This is shown in a number of ways. First, an image is usually much less detailed and consequently not as psychically engaging as a sensation; the loss of data, especially those not well attended to in the sensation from which the image originated, is apparent. Secondly, an image is psychically less intense, less vivid, less real than a sensation; this is in most cases the chief characteristic by which the image is consciously distinguished from sensation. Thirdly, an image is notably less stable than a sensation. It often wavers in the conscious field, is replaced for a while by other images, or is altered in some way under consideration. Fourthly, the perceptive range of an image is much narrower than that of a sensation. Thus in projecting an image of a clap of thunder the intensity of the sound will be equal to that projected in imagining a whisper. Fifthly, a sensation is consciously projected into space outside of the subject; an image is projected into more circumscribed inner psychic space. The most notable perceptual difference between a sensation and an image is the fact that one is conscious of the actuality, or of the capability of verification in reality of what is projected in a sensation at the precise moment of sensation, while what is projected in an image, though indeed it may be real, is not sensed as actually affecting the subject at the moment.

Psychologists have noted a general pattern regarding the reliability of reproduced material from the various senses in the imagination. Generally, visual images are more vivid and authentic than auditory, and auditory more reliable than kinesthetic. But this is obviously not always the case. Beethoven composed many of his masterpieces after he became totally deaf. Olfactory and gustatory images are the lowest of all on the scale for the general populace. But there are commercial wine and coffee tasters who can not only detect liminally nuanced differences in the material at hand, but can reproduce images of items sampled months and even years before.

The problem of hallucinations is closely associated with the question of images. In the case of an hallucination the subject loses his discriminatory ability, and mistakes an image for an actual sensation. An hallucination differs from an illusion in that the illusion merely sets forth a mistaken identification, whereas the hallucination postulates the actual existence of what is not there. An illusion differs from a delusion in that the latter is really a false belief out of keeping with an individual's intelligence, and at variance with what is commonly accepted in his cultural peer group; such a belief is sustained against all logical argument and the amassing of contrary evidence.

As the consciousness of a presence recognized as such in the absence of all external stimuli, then, hallucinations have to be carefully considered whenever there is a report of any type of extraordinary psychic phenomena.

Studies show that auditory hallucinations are the most common. After them, visual ones occur most frequently. This is, as the reader will observe, a reverse of the pattern established regarding the frequency of occurrence of images; visual images are more readily produced than auditory ones.

Our culture has bred an attitude of skepticism about unusual religious experience. Anyone who reports hearing the voice of God is immediately branded as neurotic or worse. Such people are often treated with smug superiority even by their ministers, who in their attempts to deal with the issue radiate their real conviction that what was reported could not really have happened; that their client may have been hallucinated; that the best approach to the problem is to play along so that the client will not experience further shock in his diseased condition from being told what his minister actually thinks.

Unfortunately this skeptical attitude about religious experience is one that has been cultivated by the Church itself. (There are certain exceptions where after a long time some kind of official approval is given to a religious experience, as in the case of the apparitions at Lourdes.) Such an attitude is deemed necessary to avoid superstition. It emanates from the rationalistic theology of the Middle Ages according to which logical argument is considered the only sure and safe way of contacting God. To avoid the Pelagianism that such an approach may imply, the Church has to admit the possibility of extraordinary experiences, but is reluctant to affirm that this possibility is actualized except in rare cases that can stand logical scrutiny. The gift of faith and all that flows from it are acknowledged as supernatural; but a careful distinction is made between faith as a human experience and faith as a grace. The experience, of course, is perceptible; the grace which causes it is not.

The fear of hallucination in religious experience, however, is one that can rather easily be dispelled. It may be rather hard to recognize a genuine religious experience, but it is quite easy to identify an hallucination. Current psychiatry makes this possible by providing reliable and definite criteria. The causes of hallucination are well known, and can be easily traced if one knows a bit about the life of the person who reports hearing voices or having visions. Then too, hallucinations have certain characteristics that other psychic images do not.

The etiological factors governing hallucinatory experiences are relatively few. These psychic disturbances may result from brain trauma, from certain physical ailments that affect the nervous system, from constitutional psychological states identifiable as psychoses or neuroses, from intense anxiety, from some toxic substances like alcohol or LSD injected into the system, or from prolonged deprivation or excessive excitation of the sensorium, as we mentioned before. All of these conditions are capable of diagnosis through medical examination or consideration of the general behavior of the client. It is most unlikely that a healthy and well-adjusted person who does not indulge in even an occasional alcoholic or drug binge would suffer from hallucinations.

Hallucinations are distinguishable from other sensory images. Hallucinations are almost always distorted and senseless. A patient cannot locate the object, content or data of an hallucination within his life-pattern. The person who is hallucinated will report his total experience as disturbing and unpleasant, though certain aspects of it may be fascinating and intriguing. Except for those deliberately sought through the use of drugs, people ordinarily want to rid themselves of hallucinatory experiences. And even in the case of a drug addict, it is a moot question whether what is sought and intended is an hallucinatory experience as such, or the general feeling of insouciance and euphoria that also results. In many cases of hallucination there is a generally cloudy, dreamlike condition of the consciousness; rarely is the patient fully alert and completely aware of his surroundings.

Scholastic philosophers commonly state that the human mind is unlimited in its capacity to know. Yet individuals do have very limited intelligence. This is due, these philosophers say, to the intellect's dependence upon the brain and the phantasms it produces. Thus it was thought by some scholastics that if a problem in arithmetic were clearly stated, it would eventually be solved; the only obstacle to solution that could be allowed was the inability of the mathematician to project the kind of images that would assist him. But eventually these would be found through human ingenuity, and the problem would be solved. Contemporary researchers in metalogic, however, are of the opinion that failure to solve certain mathematical problems is due not to a lack of imagination, but to the inherent limitations of both calculating machines and the human minds that create and program them. If this is true, it might lead us to suspect that we might encounter in the case of the mind as well as that of the sensorium an absolute as well as a relative or personal terminator of consciousness.

The ancient Greeks were fascinated by unsolvable problems. Zeno's famous paradox of the race between Achilles and the tortoise is a case in point. What is suggested is that if the tortoise is given a lead one can never prove that Achilles will be able to overtake the animal, though common sense indicates that he will. For by the time Achilles reaches the starting point of the tortoise, let us say point alpha, the beast will have proceeded to point beta, and by the time Achilles reaches that, the tortoise will be at point gamma, and so on. From similar considerations in more recent times Cantor has constructed a set theory about natural, rational, and real numbers that contradicts the ancient Greek notion that the whole is greater than its parts, but equal to the sum of them.

In the area of logic too the ancient Greeks posed some insoluble problems. One of them surfaced in an alleged argument between Protagoras and Euathlus. Protagoras contracted to be Euathlus' law professor if Euathlus would pay him one-half of his fee immediately and the other half after he won his first case. But Euathlus never went into practice. When Protagoras sued for the second half of his fee, he argued in this way: Euathlus contends that he need not pay me; but he is wrong. If he wins this case, then by virtue of our agreement he must pay. But if, on the other hand, he loses this case, then by the judgment of this court he must pay me. In either case, therefore, he must pay. Euathlus, however, argued in this way: Protagoras is wrong when he says that I must pay him. If he wins this case, I will have lost, and then by our agreement no payment is necessary. If, on the other hand, he loses this case, then by the judgment of this court I am absolved from paying him. In either case, then, I do not have to pay him. Closer to our times Bertrand Russell proposed a similar unsolvable paradox about sets that do not contain themselves.

With the advent of non-Euclidian geometry pioneered by men like Gauss and Lobachevsky a whole host of insoluble problems resulting from the relationship of our quadridimensional universe with other totally disparate systems appeared, and highlighted the seemingly inherent inability of the human mind to cope with them. So too problems about the infinite and the infinite series posed by Cantor, Russell and others seem to indicate that man simply does not have a sufficient consciousness to solve them. One example will suffice to illustrate this kind of problem. A perfect number is any natural one which, excluding itself, is equal to the sum of its possible natural divisors. The number 6 is the smallest of these. Six is divisible by 1, 2, and 3. And $1+2+3=6$. Other perfect numbers in the series are 28, 496, 8128, etc. The problem is to determine whether there is a finite or infinite series of them.

The issue of the terminator of mental consciousness is also important in explaining the possibility of creative insight. Experience shows that at times a person is able to transcend the limen of his intellectual awareness with surprising inventive results. A story illustrating this fact is told about Elias Howe, the inventor of the sewing machine. He worked out all the details of the mechanism with the result that he had a device that could stitch better and faster than any human hand. But there was one great problem. He had used a conventional needle with its eyelet at the blunt end. No matter how hard he tried he could not prevent the thread from tangling. The faster the machine worked, the greater mess of thread it produced. Ultimately Howe was exhausted by his efforts. It just seemed to him impossible to solve this difficulty. When he could work no longer, he fell exhausted on his bed, and dropped off to sleep immediately. While sleeping he had a vivid dream. He found himself in a strange, primitive land inhabited by savages armed with long spears. Since he was defenseless, he was easily captured by the natives and brought before their chief. He was accused of being a foreign invader and condemned to death. The natives took him and tied him to a stake. An execution squad then raised its spears and was about to strike. He suddenly awoke with one element of the dream still fixed firmly in his mind. He had observed that the spears of the natives had holes just beyond the razor-sharp points. He rushed into his workshop and made a needle with an eyelet near the point, inserted it into his machine, and found that it worked perfectly.

The terminator of mental consciousness is often a factor even in quite ordinary thinking processes. Very often I am not able to account for my ideas. Many times I can see how they are connected with previous experience, with current activities or interests, with the general thrust of my life. But at times there spring into my mind ideas and even complex reasoning processes, the antecedents of which I am not at all able to identify. Sometimes these can become obsessive ideas, or notions that can change my whole basic mental orientation. Neither modern psychology nor ancient philosophy has solved the mystery of how thought sometimes emerges suddenly from the totally unconscious.

The limina of memory are fairly well marked off in the various laws of association and disassociation with which the modern psychologist is familiar. The factors involved in fixing experience in the memory are quite well known. Chief among these is the intensity of the original impression. The more intense the impression an experience makes, generally speaking, the better it will be retained by the memory. The intensity of an original impression will be gauged from both the striking quality of the object perceived and the mood of the subject at the time of the experience. Attention is another important factor in retention. It will be harder to remember data to which minimal attention is paid than those which are the principal objects of concentration. Again, the clearer and simpler the object, the more easily it will be remembered. The physiological state of the memorizer also enters into consideration. Bad digestion, for example, inhibits one's capacity to retain, as does also strong emotion. Obviously, one's motivation in learning plays an important part. A speaker more readily memorizes a piece for a larger stipend than for a smaller one. Memorizing is facilitated if the material to be learned is well organized; random data cannot be recalled as easily. The thrust of the higher functions of consciousness is toward order. Repetition, as is evident, plays an important role in recall. Generally speaking, the more a person repeats to himself the data to be memorized, the better grasp he will have on it. In this area, however, one can discover another limen. Too frequent a repetition of the material to be learned may eventually lead to a mental block which will inhibit retention entirely. Researches in the area of repetition indicate that the speed and rhythm, a holistic or divided approach, visual or auditory emphases are all factors to be considered, but ones which may vary considerably from person to person.

As in the case of creative ideas, it is sometimes hard to say just what brings an impression stored in the memory, perhaps for many years, into the light of consciousness. Various theories of retention and stimulation have been proposed. But it seems clear that all of them that are plausible recognize the ability of the subject to reach in some way beyond the terminator of his consciousness and draw into the conscious field what was buried, if not in the unconscious, at least in the dark area of awareness. The laws of memory which we have briefly considered show us how to facilitate the conscious mind's accomplishment of this feat, but they do not indicate by what power or precisely how this is done.

Even where the connection between what one is conscious of and a former experience that was buried in the memory is clear, the process of recall is still quite mysterious, involving as it does the drawing into the field of full consciousness of material that was a second before in no way conscious.

Consideration of the operation of memory in the conscious life raises the issue of whether there is actually a multiplicity of conscious limina in this faculty. Three horizons seem to appear when we examine the scope of our memory. We are aware of what we definitely know and can recall at will. Right now I am not thinking of the propositions in the Apostles' creed. But I know that I could recite the full formula if someone asked me to do so. So I am sure both that I know it and can recall it. Secondly, we seem to be aware of what we have known and do now in some way recognize as familiar, but are not able to recall with precision without some additional help. When asked for the name of a great pioneer in intelligence testing, I am sure that I know one. I would say that his name is on the tip of my tongue, but right now it is blocked in my memory. I can use some device to assist recall. Does the name begin with an A? No. With a B? Yes, I am sure it begins with a B. Is it an Italian name? German? French? Yes, that's it. A French name beginning with a B. Of course, Binet. Thirdly, we are aware of what we never knew, or are at least in no way conscious of. If someone asks me for any one of the Arabic words for camel, I am sure that right now I cannot respond, and there is absolutely no use in searching my memory for a response.

The second horizon, when we are aware that we know something, but cannot now bring it fully into consciousness, is most intriguing because it focusses our attention into the dark area of our awareness, an area which seems to be so full of surprising and creative potential. The third horizon, too, brings light to bear on the same area with a resulting conviction that what is being searched out there is not present.

The process of forgetting is as interesting as that of remembering. Forgetting is almost as essential to psychic well-balance as remembering. If we forgot nothing, our minds would be cluttered up with scads of useless data that might well impede the possibility of focussing our attention on what we want to consider. Data which were not fixed in the center of consciousness in the initial experience are those which tend to be forgotten first of all. Those that were of no great interest, that did not stimulate us are the most likely to pass into complete oblivion beyond any possibility of recall. Time also, of course, is an important factor, and, in general, the longer the time lapse between the original experience and the attempt to recall it, the more difficult recall will be. Repetition is another factor that has to be considered. The forgetting index varies in inverse proportion to the frequency of repetition. Purely psychological or ego-based influences like repression also radically affect one's power to forget. Experiences that are embarrassing or unpleasant tend to be forgotten more readily than those that are pleasant and gratifying.

In the area of memory we find the terminator of consciousness to be highly motile. Our brief consideration of some of the factors influencing its position relative to the conscious life revealed a few of the basic laboratory findings. But, of course, we must also recognize the fact that there are many other highly personal and idiosyncratic patterns that are equally important for the individual, but hard to identify or classify.

The condition of amnesia shows the possibility of a highly centripetal movement of the terminator of consciousness, while that of hypermnesia evidences a centrifugal tendency that enlarges immensely the field of consciousness in this area. Masserman, in his *Principles of Dynamic Psychiatry,* records the case of a woman who, after being separated from her family for four years, insisted not only that she had never met her husband and children before, but that she was really not the person whom they claimed her to be. On the other hand, the memory feats of a prodigy like Cardinal Mezzofanti are well known. As a boy he learned to speak fluently languages like Latin, Greek, Spanish and Swedish. In his early youth he mastered Hebrew, Arabic, and several other oriental languages. In full maturity he could, it is said, speak about forty languages, could read and understand about thirty more, and was in some way familiar with about forty-five additional dialects.

There can be no doubt that all of the factors of psychic life that we have considered thus far can be at least to some small degree influenced by the emotional state of the individual. This is true even of the sensorium. The term "blind rage" is surely more than a metaphor. When I am extremely angry I often miss vital cues that I would easily pick up if I were not under excessive emotional stress. The emotions not only affect my state of consciousness in general and the various sensory and mental data within its field, but they exert an important influence on the physical condition of the organism, and, in turn, are themselves highly nuanced by it. This mutual relationship between emotion and the condition of the body and its various organs is called by psychologists somatic resonance.

Everyone knows the connection between peptic ulcers and personality. In general, it is the emotionally active, tall, asthenic individual who is much more susceptible than the stocky, extroverted, pyknic type. Invariably a tranquilizer or anticholinergic drug to block excitation of the ulcer by the autonomic nervous system will be part of the medical regimen. Emotional states are not only responsible for pathological conditions; they also can influence the regular functioning of the digestive system; some individuals are, of course, more sensitive in this regard than others. People who are excited or irritated in this way complain that they have butterflies in their stomach.

Some of the other somatic effects of emotional excitement are also well known. The heart will pound. The face will become flushed. Muscles will be tensed. The breathing rate will increase. The hands may tremble; the palms will become sweaty. The throat and mouth will become dry. Urination may occur more frequently. Eventually the whole body may be bathed in a cold sweat. One may feel weak or faint. Even after the excitement wanes, it leaves its mark upon the body. Many people after an emotional bout feel tired out; some are completely fatigued. Others feel restless or depressed. Some become more irritable and jumpy. Others suffer from anorexia, insomnia, or are apt to have frightening dreams.

Conversely, there are various somatic factors that deeply affect conscious emotional life. We are especially interested in them because they provide additional evidence for the fact that our conscious life can be nuanced by agents that are totally unconscious, or in the dark area of our awareness.

The generally euphoric feeling of the healthy individual facilitates and encourages pleasant emotional states. On the other hand, somatic disease very often leads to depression, irritability, languor, or insouciance. Kübler-Ross in her book *On Death and Dying* outlines six definite emotional states in the person who becomes aware of impending death. More specifically, certain physiological conditions, like blood volume in a particular organ, heart action, the status of the bowels and bladder, engorgement of the seminal vesicles, ovulation, menstruation, etc. are all known to exert an influence on emotional life. The hormones and chalones produced by the endocrine and other glands also affect conscious life. Yet in many of these instances there is absolutely no awareness of the somatic condition that produces a definite mood or emotion. Addison's disease, associated with a hypofunction of the adrenal cortex, produces psychic symptoms like extreme fatigue, confusion and patent emotional instability. Disturbances of the pituitary gland may result in "emotional hallucinations," for instance, unprovoked and uncontrollable anger and rage.

The awareness we have of a difference between free and responsible action on the one hand, and compulsive or spontaneous behavior on the other, leads us to believe that there is also some kind of terminator in volition. The range of intensity of will action also confirms this suspicion. The existence of abulia, or complete lack of decisive power, in some individuals points to a centrifugal movement of the terminator, while feats of great will power evidence a centripetal motion of the terminator in others.

The will exerts a definite influence over other psychic functions. In controlling the direction of consciousness itself, the will plays an extremely important part in setting the position of the terminator in other faculties. The will has a more or less direct control over some organic functions, like the fields of vision and the gustatory sense. I can direct my eyes where I like, and eat what I want. Over other functions the will has only an indirect rule. I cannot fully control my affective states. Sometimes I cannot help but laugh or cry. However, through the entertainment of distractions or the mechanism of setting up opposite external behavior, I can exert some control even over my emotions. I can smile through my tears, or turn my attention to some other thing I am interested in when experiencing sexual passion. Of particular interest is the will's influence over the memory. Here full control cannot always be achieved. But very often I can summon up stored data and associate them with a current train of thought. It is really the will in this case that prompts transcendence of the terminator of consciousness to bring into the field of complete awareness material that lies in the dark area of the memory. Very often a general assessment of psychic response is made in terms of characteristic will operation. Thus people will be classified as impetuous or phlegmatic, weak or strong, followers or leaders in accordance with the usual mode in which they are wont to make decisions.

The fact that the will can be trained indicates a certain flexibility in the terminator of decision. It can be extended or retracted. Since, however, the will is usually viewed as a "blind" faculty, following as it does the judgment of the intellect, the position of the terminator of mental consciousness may be a more important factor in the exercise of the decision-making faculty. One may detect a mutual causal influence at work between the terminator of decision and the terminator of consciousness.

If criteria are to be set up to assist identifying a particular experience as one connected with grace or God, we must presuppose experiences can be communicated in some way or other. The question of communication of experience is, however, one of the most difficult and complicated in all psychology. The fact that psychic laws have been established and recognized by reputable scientists shows not only that some valid external expression of experience is feasible, but also that it can be subjected to rigorous scientific control. Indeed, an unarticulated presupposition of all psychotherapy is an acknowledgment of the fact of valid communication of experiential material between patient and doctor. The best historical sources we have are accounts of experiences. To be sure, the possibility of communicating our experiences authentically is so much a part of our lives and so intimately bound up with ordinary discourse that it is simply taken for granted. It would defy the imagination to picture a day in our life which would be bereft of all types of experiential communication. Human experience is so interesting and intriguing that the theatrical arts, the movies and television entertainment are mostly taken up with it.

Yet despite all of this, it is a fact that we cannot really communicate our experience to others. As we already indicated, experience is such a highly personal property of our existence that, like personhood itself, it is incommunicable.

I cannot really explain to others who I am. I may have a pretty good grasp of my own identity in my own mind, but let me try to explain my own individual, unique, irreplaceable and definitely identifiable selfhood to someone else! It just cannot be done. Nor can I fully identify my consciousness for someone else, nor what flows from it, my experience. At best, I can presume that the other person has a similar identity, consciousness and experience. Thus he in general, *mutatis mutandis,* is aware from his own identity, consciousness and experience of what I am talking about. To be sure, he will presume that I too as a person enjoy similar prerogatives. But the point is that he will be able to understand my identity, consciousness and experience only in terms of his own, by using his own as a basic reference point, namely by keeping in mind that mine are actually different from his, though he can presume them to be somewhat similar. The symbols by which I try to communicate some understanding of my experience to him, be they verbal or non-verbal or both, serve at best to arouse a recall of his own experience, which he judges to be similar to mine. At least, he will be confident that it is similar because he has associated the words or signs I used with certain elements of his experience and has presumed that I have done the same.

Basically then faith or trust must lie at the very roots of the issue of communication of experience. To understand what you are talking about when you tell me of your experience I must believe, without any possibility of actual verification by means of scientific proof or personal experiential contact, in a number of things. First, I must believe that what you are relating is really your experience and not a story you made up. Your experience is so personal and subjective that it is impossible for me to check it. Certainly I could ask others to confirm the fact that you were actually in the circumstances you describe. But no one else could tell me how they affected you, how you viewed them, how you felt, what decisions you made. Secondly, I must believe that the signs and words you use to communicate your experience to me are the ones that best make me understand what your experience must have been like. Thirdly, I must believe that, though we grew up separately, our past experience has had enough common elements to allow me to endow the symbols you use in relating your experience with the same sentient content that you attach to them. And fourthly, I must believe that, though my experience and your experience are uniquely different so that mine could never be identical with yours, we have enough in common to permit me to empathize with you, to make you a double of me, to place myself in your position and try to be you as you were experiencing what you are telling me about. To do this I must feel with you as you relate your experience, but more importantly, I must try to project how you felt as you were having your experience. I must experience in my imagination the very same thing you experienced. I must experience vicariously through my empathic projection what you experienced really.

Quite obviously what you relate to me cannot be descriptive of your total experience. If you were to describe the full content of just a single percept you had during your experience, the data might fill a fair-sized book. And even then you probably would not be giving me a complete account of what you were aware of only peripherally, or what was also experienced in the dark area of your consciousness. I would have to understand that the material you present to me as your experience is highly selective if I am to appreciate exactly what you are recounting for me. It is the material you reflected on and found most significant. In recalling the experience you determined what was important for you, and now while telling me about your experience you presume that these same data will be significant for me, whether this is actually true or not. Moreover, since what you are presenting is really reflective material, it is actually a recounting of your experience, and consequently not a version of it that is unalloyed or untouched by subsequent experience. In other words, what you are relaying to me is your present experience of a past experience; and this present experience is one that has captured the past precisely as modified by a whole series of other experiences that have intervened between your original experience and the current communication of it. It is this fact that might prove an obstacle to my faith in your ability to tell me really what originally happened to you exactly as it happened. Only my own empathy can save me from a certain amount of doubt, and where it is blocked or rendered weak and ineffectual, no reliable communication can be had.

In the communication of an experience, then, there is considerable risk of misplaced faith, and this hazard becomes greater as an experience is relayed from person to person. True, people are preconditioned to have faith in the reported experience of others; they tend generally more to believe than to disbelieve, to accept more than to reject when what is proposed is the experience of another. The word itself seems to have a magic hold on the faith of people. While one might lean toward skepticism in regard to data I present in communicating a scientific fact, or an historical situation, one would be more likely to believe without questioning my experiences. Thus if I were to tell you that vanilla extract comes from the pods and not the roots of an orchid-like plant, you would probably check it out in an encyclopedia before accepting my word. You would do the same if I told you that the difference in our words for meat on the hoof: cow, sheep and pig (from Saxon antecedents) and meat on the table: beef, mutton and pork (from French roots) was due to the historical contingency of the Norman invasion of England. The conquering French sat at table while the conquered Saxons tended their herds for them. But if I were to tell you that I have a headache, you would accept my statement without question.

A television program aired some years ago took issue with the reliability of relayed experiential information. The viewing audience as well as a student from a midwestern university were made witnesses to a murder scene on a crowded train.

Everyone clearly saw who the murderer was, how he was dressed, how he approached his victim and what kind of weapon he used. The student who witnessed the enactment was then asked to describe his experience to another student, and he to another, and so on until the experiment was concluded with a sixth student. This last person was then asked to recount for the television viewers what had happened. It was patent that in the telling and passing on of information, due to both selection and subjective emphasis, great distortions regarding the sex of the murderer, his description, the situation of the victim and the type of weapon used had crept into the story. In fact, there was some question as to whether the act was one of murder or self defense. Yet each student to whom the information was relayed accepted the relator's account in faith without challenge.

Law courts have long been concerned about the issue of faith in recounted experience. Here, because of the importance of testimony in relation to the freedom or even the life of the accused, a greater attempt is made to insure the trustworthiness of accounts given of personal experience. The witness is at least put under oath to focus attention upon the significance of his testimony. Today he places his hand upon the Bible to show that he is conscious of the fact that his retelling of his experience will have some effect not only upon his fellow human, for whom he must have some concern, but also upon his own future, and indeed, if he is a believer, upon his eternal salvation. The Bible seems to indicate that in ancient times the hand of a witness was placed upon his thigh. And, of course, this would make no sense at all. The scriptures have obviously been bowdlerized. A witness in ancient times put his hand on his testicles. That is why his statement is called testimony and his act testifying. And this is also why women were not admitted as witnesses in the ancient and medieval courts. Women involved in litigation had to get a male champion or sponsor to testify for them. The idea that the ancients had was that in testifying a person accepted responsibility for the future. The future generation was seen to be potentially enclosed in the testicles of the witness. So the account he gave of his experience was considered more credible if he was fully aware not only of what had happened in the past, but also of the relationship of these data to the future. For it was not just the general tendency of people to accept experiential reports on faith that was to be the basis of the court's acceptance of testimony, but the sense of responsibility for the future evidenced by a witness. What was past was done; but the future was yet to be lived. And the decision of the court was more significant for the future than it was for the past.

Unfortunately, however, in the relating of religious experience as time passed little attention was paid to such a guarantor of fidelity. Reliance was placed on the general sense of trust in experiential accounts. So the stories of the experiences of the martyrs, or those who had witnessed their sufferings, eventually became grossly exaggerated. Fantastic legends were created. As the stories were retold distortions became more and more frequent. This was due not only to the limitations of memory, but also to an avid desire to create heroes. Heavenly patrons of countries, towns, families or individuals had to be the saints most favored by God, and had to outstrip in their feats of bravado and their miracles the patrons of rivals. The martyrs thus were robbed of their individuality and historicity in order that a more vivid and ideal portrait of them might be passed down to their admirers. They became abstractions instead of real people. The stories about them became cyclic, transhistorical, static. The tendency to generalize was detected by later researchers in the similarity of accounts in the purported life stories of different heroes. Take, for instance, the incident that was supposed to have happened to St. Genesius, a martyr now proven to have been a purely legendary figure. He was a comedian in the court of an important pagan official. He found his audience particularly responsive to his incisive mockery of the Christian liturgical rites. One day while the mimic was lampooning baptism he was suddenly converted, professed his belief before the magistrate and was condemned to death. The same story is told in various connections of at least three other early Christian martyrs. The human and prosaic fades quickly from the stories of the saints; what the populace desires to hear about is the divine and miraculous. So the legends of the martyrs became cluttered with accounts of exaggerated and futile miracles, with contradictions and anachronisms, with childish oversimplifications. Sometimes even the hero or heroine was the product of a desire to explain the existence of a particular church or shrine, there being no historical evidence whatsoever of the fact that such a person ever existed. One has only to think of the cases of St. Philomena and St. Photina. When the Bollandists set out to rid the legends of the saints of unprovable, unhistorical data in the late sixteenth century they faced a monumental task that has not been completed even to this day. When Heribert Rosweyde of the Jesuit College at Douai first proposed his plan to purify hagiography of spurious material to Cardinal Bellarmine, the latter remarked to a colleague: "This man counts on living for two hundred years!" But the Cardinal himself did not know the full extent of the task.

The Church, of course, is not the only myth-maker. Propagandists of all kinds capitalize on the inclination of people to apotheosize. Sometimes, as was the case with Stalin in Russia, heroes are established or discredited at the whim of a governmental regime. At times historians themselves play a major role in distorting experiential evidence to prove a pet theory.

The pendulum swings to extremes before it comes to rest in the middle. If the Church of the past was patently gullible in accepting spurious religious experience, the Church of more recent times has been overly skeptical in judging reports of extraordinary religious phenomena. There is a bias against believing stories of an encounter with the divine that has discouraged people from telling even their pastors about any kind of unusual religious experience.

Obviously it is difficult to set down any norms about the communication of religious experience. But to pursue the objective of this essay it is necessary to have some rule of thumb, some guidelines that are usually applicable, though they may not work in each and every individual case.

First, we must deal with the time factor as it affects accounts of ordinary and extraordinary religious experiences. In regard to accounts remote in time there is a tendency to disregard ordinary experience, not because it is not believed, but because it is seen to be insignificant. On the other hand, one observes a tendency not only to believe, but also to enhance and embellish extraordinary experience, to supply detail where it may be lacking. Conversely, with contemporary religious experience, ordinary accounts engender belief and empathy. Individuals are prone to compare the stories of others with their own experience, and if some similarity is noted, understanding and acceptance will ensue. There is a reluctance, however, to subscribe to a description of extraordinary phenomena as precisely religious in tenor, though they may be regarded readily as psychological aberrations. The listener will be skeptical for he will presume that he has had no extraordinary religious experiences himself. Hence he will have no basis of comparison. He will not be able fully to comprehend the experience that is related to him. He will not be able to empathize. So he will be loathe to believe. He might well be tolerant and sympathetic. He might play along with the relator. But there will be no real communication because there is no common ground and no faith.

Secondly, the way of speaking about an experience profoundly affects one's ability to communicate it. Detailed descriptions tend to reinforce faith and empathy when there is question of ordinary religious experience. Perhaps the reason is that if any one detail sounds strange and fails to arouse empathy, the odds are that others will. As we said, the success of communication of an experience depends upon the amount of empathy it produces. The more a person tells about his experience, provided that what he relates is common to the experience of all, the more it is likely to be perceived to jibe with and reflect the experience of the hearer. Thus belief in the account is rendered more secure.

On the other hand, detail in the relating of an extraordinary experience inhibits empathy. If what is told remains vague, general and mysterious, it will strike a chord of recognition in the consciousness of listeners, because everyone has had or thinks he has had, an experience that is somewhat numinal. But credibility decreases with the vividness of the account, because singular or unique aspects of the experience, precisely because they are so highly personal, are not only basically ineffable so that words will really fail to communicate them, but also so different from the experience of hearers that a reference point for recognition will be lacking. At best the listener can only appeal to some other similar account that he has read or heard about. But this forms a poor basis for empathy, and will bring epistemological or psychological questions to the fore.

Thirdly, the general relationship of the relator to the listener is paramount for the communication of extraordinary experience. Where a mutual atmosphere of faith and trust already exists, where the persons involved in the communication are well known to each other, there is not much danger that the listener will interpret unusual experience as psychotic behavior, nor, on the other hand, will the relator be reluctant to express just what he felt for fear that he will be branded as a mental case. If, however, the parties involved are complete strangers, there will be no secure index by which the hearer can judge the authenticity of the account, nor any assurance on the part of the relator that his story will be received with openness and sympathy. An obvious exception, however, might be noted in the case of the minister or priest. Here the relator might well think that because of his role the ecclesiastic would be inclined to listen to him and believe him, and perhaps even give him some help in handling extraordinary religious experience. But of course, many who have reasoned in this way soon saw their mistake when they were turned off, advised to see a psychiatrist, or told rather bluntly that God does not act in such ways.

Since communication of religious experience is inherently difficult and often complicated by the fear of embarrassment, it will have its best prospects of being effective, in general, under the following conditions. First, there must be some degree of mutual understanding of the symbol systems of the persons involved. This means that the listener must not only know what the words the relator uses mean in general, but especially what connotation they have for him. The listener must also be aware of other signs and cues given by the relator that will help in the interpretation of his experience. Secondly, there must prevail an atmosphere not only of openness, but even of faith, trust and empathy between the communicators. Empathy, as we have explained, does not mean mere tolerance or sympathy; it denotes a total subjective effort to try to have vicariously through the influence of the words and actions of the relator in the hearer's own imagination the very experience of the relator to the extent that it is possible. Thirdly, the listener must have forbearance enough to refrain from hasty judgments about the experience of the relator. The same caution is advised in regard to the setting up of tests, unless the relator himself is in doubt about his experience. Fourthly, the listener must be convinced that he will never be able to appreciate the experience of the relator exactly as he does. So the listener must will to let it be as it is. He should hold back any desire to modify or recast the relator's account, or retell it in the light of his own experience. If clarifications are necessary, questions are the best way to get them. Lastly, the listener must be aware that what the relator is presenting is not his experience itself, but his reflections upon it, reflections that may have already changed and modified it, reflections that present only significant selections from the total experience that the relator had, reflections that may imply certain value judgments made about it, that may reveal certain doubts or questions on the one hand, or a degree of certitude on the other which were not part of the original experience.

The fourth general rule of thumb to be applied to the question of communicating an experience is that continual extraordinary experience, because it involves a repositioning and extension of the terminator of consciousness, may bring about an altered consciousness, the effects of which may become apparent in behavior. This may become a problem for those listeners who are well acquainted with the relator. The quality of consciousness may vary from generation to generation. The reason that parents today may not be able to understand the antics of their adolescent children may well be more fundamental than is commonly realized. Objective reasons can be adduced, and they are well known. But there might also be another factor involved that is not fully appreciated because it is highly subjective. McLuhan has pointed out how the media today are really extenders of consciousness. Consciousness itself today differs considerably from what it was one hundred years ago. The change has been quite gradual, and so has not been too perceptible. But as time passes change will occur more rapidly. It will then become more noticeable. Today the behavioral effects of extended consciousness are easy to delineate; tomorrow extended consciousness itself will become a factor to be examined, evaluated and explained.

The same phenomenon takes place in the case of extraordinary experience. Consciousness itself is extended or altered, and this change has to be taken into account when an attempt is made to communicate what is experienced. Unless this fact is borne in mind by the listener, he will not have the openminded attitude that is required for any kind of effective communication of extraordinary experience.

In this chapter we have been laying the psychological foundation for the hypothesis concerning religious experience that we shall advance later. We have tried to marshal some evidence for the fact that the human organism is capable at almost every level of its psychic operation to transcend the terminator of consciousness, and in some way to contact what lies in the shadowy region beyond. Indeed in some areas, as for instance that of memory, this capability is so much part and parcel of daily living that it is taken for granted.

In contending that this dark area of human consciousness can have some influence upon experience, an influence that can be surfaced at times by reflection, we are not proposing any new psychological doctrine. Subliminally conscious experience has long been the subject of much research. But recent studies, as we saw, have revealed more completely the full range of this kind of experience within the psyche and the real nature of its influence on conscious life. We would prefer to refer to experiential data in the dark area of consciousness by using the term "transliminally conscious" rather than "subliminal" to emphasize the fact that they normally lie beyond the range of consciousness, but can in some way be reached through reflection; but we do not want to give the impression that they were at one time fully conscious, and now cannot be reached only because they have slipped below the conscious level; they may never have been fully conscious, and may never be fully conscious; nor do we want to give the impression that they are too weak as stimuli to break through the threshold of consciousness; they may be in themselves most powerful and compelling. That is why we prefer to call them transliminal rather than subliminal.

The rest of this book will be devoted to the study of transliminal factors in human peak and religious experience.

3

PEAK EXPERIENCE

If we can establish contact with God anywhere within the range of human experience, we might well suspect that the most likely place to search for it would be in the area of peak experience. By peak experience we would mean that which is particularly striking and significant. It is the type of experience that we cannot easily forget because it was so unusual or different. Peak experiences are those which bring about notable changes in behavior, changes that are profound and lasting. From a peak experience a person might well develop a whole new outlook on life, a different or more meaningful philosophy.

We generally tend to look upon a peak experience as a sudden, startling, totally unexpected happening in our lives. But it is possible that its onset and development will be more insidious. A peak experience could gradually evolve slowly and imperceptibly, consuming many years between its initial and final stages. In this sense faith might fall within the scope of peak experiences, and thus pertain to the ambit of inquiry in this chapter. When one is unhorsed, is blinded and hears a mysterious voice as St. Paul did, he might well consider his encounter with God as a peak experience. All of this occurred in a very short time, suddenly and unexpectedly. But the time factor is really not that important. A gradual growth in Christian living might also be described as a peak experience of faith. And we do not wish to deny this fact, though in this chapter for the sake of clarity we shall be referring chiefly to those experiences which are more unusual and striking. But what we say of the sudden, intensely concentrated, fulminating kind of peak experience can also be applied, *mutatis mutandis,* to the more prolonged, insidiously evolving, less conspicious type.

In the previous chapter the first thing that we noted about experience is that it is highly personal and unique. When we considered the possibility of communication of experience we proposed the idea that as such experience is fully ineffable. But since there are certain common elements, and since a selection of these can be made for communication, some possibility remains of classifying and discussing certain characteristics of human experience. We must presume that this is valid even for peak experience, where uniqueness and ineffability are paramount features.

The first overall and distinctive characteristic of peak experience that we can note is that it often incorporates within itself a union of opposites. What might separately be perceived as contradictory elements can be reconciled in and made a part of a peak experience. It is precisely this fact that highlights the peak experience as a kind of transcendence. And the notion of transcendence must play an important part in any theological analysis of experience. The theology of the past recognized the significance of the phenomenon of union of opposites in the experience of conversion. It teaches that the justified person is *simul justus et peccator,* at one and the same time both just and a sinner. In Catholic theology this notion, at least since the time of Luther, has been toned down and modified. Some authors redefine it to mean *simul justus et peccabilis;* that is, the person who is justified remains liable to sin. The mystery of sin still has hold of him in that original sin has so darkened his intellect and weakened his will that unless he receives an extraordinary grace he will not be able to refrain from sinning venially. And even his justified condition does not assure him of final perseverance. Then too, though he is truly just in the eyes of God he must continue, as the Mass liturgy itself now more clearly indicates, to repent of his past sins.

In Protestantism, on the other hand, the phrase *simul justus et peccator* is often interpreted to mean that the person who is justified by faith has no merit, no good works, nothing of his own before God but sin. What was wrought in him is due to God alone, and remains God's work so that he can claim no credit for it himself.

Undoubtedly, these two positions can in large part be reconciled, since the Roman Catholic too must acknowledge justification as the entirely gratuitous gift of God. Whatsoever theological explanation might be advanced, however, on the experiential level, both Catholic and Protestant have to agree that the justified person feels that he is at one and the same time righteous, and still in some sense sinful. Thus the experience of justification entails a kind of union of opposites. And the transcendence of sin perceived through faith and trust is achieved from the human standpoint precisely through the acknowledgment of one's sinful condition.

The Christian very commonly experiences the knitting together in his life of both limitation and marvelous transcendence. The experience undoubtedly has its prototype and origin in the paschal mystery itself. It was precisely by accepting his passion and death that Jesus attained the transcendence of the resurrection. Christ's humanity itself became the instrument of salvation and glorification. The paradox of the cross is not the only one set forth in New Testament literature. The weak and little things, the things that are of no account in the world's estimation are the ones chosen by God to accomplish his will. Pride will fall; humility will assure exaltation. The first shall be last and the last first. The harlot and publican will precede the Pharisee in the kingdom. The poor Lazarus will repose in the bosom of Abraham while Dives languishes in everlasting torment.

The true ideal of the Christian has been set forth by spiritual theology as one encompassing self-abasement and mortification. One secures eternal treasures only by limiting earthly desires and forsaking fleshly pursuits. With the example of

Jesus' paschal mystery set before him as a model, and the gospel paradoxes ringing in his ears, the Christian ascetic was called forth to embark on a great adventure. He was summoned to a peak experience. Nor was the ecstasy he was to feel in the accomplishment of his task a morbid, masochistic pleasure; it was the kind of self-fulfillment that could come to him only through the assurance of an unshakable faith, a belief that he was actually on the way to a final destiny that exceeded in grandeur the capabilities of the human imagination. And the fact that this pursuit of transcendence through limitation constituted a peak experience for many saints of the Church in past eras cannot be gainsaid.

The way of paradox and contradiction is well known in Zen Buddhism and Islamic ascetical literature and proceeds along parallel lines. In Zen, however, the limitation is imposed not chiefly on the flesh, but on the contemplative mind, and the resultant breakthrough in experience is perceived as *satori*, or true enlightenment. One finds in both Moslem and Buddhist literature the story of the child who approached a wise man with a lighted torch in his hand. Upon being asked where the flame came from, the child promptly blew it out, and replied: "Tell me where it has gone, and I will tell you where it came from."

In peak experience other than those of a religious nature, this phenomenon of union of opposites is also often discernable. A peak experience may begin with a subjective mood of helplessness, anger or frustration: a feeling that one simply lacks control over the various vicissitudes of life; one is often convinced in his own mind that things are really "beyond me." Very often this feeling will occur when one is facing the impending death of a relative or friend, or sometimes that even of a complete stranger for whom one senses some responsibility or concern. Or it may take place when one receives news that he has an incurable sickness, or when one's means of livelihood are cut off. But soon this feeling is coupled with one of exhilaration. One senses also an air of confidence; one per-

ceives a kind of surge of power from within; one has an awareness of success, an assurance of eventually overcoming any
obstacle. And even if the worst happens, it will be borne better
because of the offsetting transcendent mood.

The same kind of peak experience, often in reverse order,
can emanate from love. One feels transported, exhilarated,
suffused with new energy, a zest for life, a persuasion that one
can really do anything or dare anything for the sake of love.
Yet at the same time one is aware of one's basic helplessness
in the situation. How can I really express what I feel? What
can I do to prove my love? What if I am rejected? Can I over-
come all the obstacles that I will encounter in the pursuit of
my love?

The anger, the frustration, the helplessness that is felt in
a peak experience is often of the free-floating variety. That is,
I am not always able to definitely locate in my consciousness
the real object of these emotions. I cannot always assign a
cause; I cannot always successfully analyze what I experience.
The same is often true of the opposite feeling of exhilaration,
of joy, of power, the assurance of success.

The following account was given by a seminarian working
as an orderly in a large hospital. He encountered an old man
with a terminal disease in one of the wards. The seminarian
became concerned about him because he seemed to be completely abandoned. He had no visitors and no friends in the
hospital. He was dying a slow and lonely death. The man was
not very communicative, but on occasions the seminarian tried
to talk with him. One day he noted that the man was definitely
in trouble. He sounded a medical alarm, and about fifteen
members of the staff responded. Soon the man's bed was sur-
rounded with a maze of technical gear, as defibrillators, tra-
cheotomy trays, oxygen masks and giant syringes were rushed
to the spot. Doctors pounded, punctured and shocked the poor
victim. But it was all to no avail. The doctor in charge indicated no more could be done; the patient's heart had been stilled
for too long a time. As suddenly as the staff members had ap-

peared, they now dispersed to continue their routine tasks. The body was left for the orderly to cover and deposit in the morgue. As he was observing the proceedings, the seminarian felt an overwhelming sense of anger, frustration and helplessness. He knew that all the forces of modern medical technology had been marshalled to aid this unfortunate man; yet they were ineffectual. He really did not know why he was angry; his ire was not directed at the doctors, nurses or even the equipment. But as he prepared the body, out of his frustration there came a new insight into the meaning of death. As he looked into the face of the deceased, he thought he perceived a look of peace, quiet and contentment. And it was so unusual on the face of one who had suffered so much. After all his trials this old man was now truly at rest. Death brings a surcease of agony, humiliation and turmoil. Together with his anger, the seminarian also experienced some of that peace which he seemed to perceive in the features of the dead man. For him this was a peak experience, for not only was it an incident that he would never forget, but as the result of this encounter with death he felt that he would in the future be better able to cope with it. When the time came for his parents and friends to die, when indeed he would himself face death, he knew he would be able to view it in a new light. He would see it as a release. Death would always be for him the way to true peace.

Sometimes the opposite emotions felt in a peak experience seem to cause a split in the very personhood of the individual undergoing it. A person seems to be at one and the same time both himself and other to himself.

Another seminarian relates his experience when he received the news that his father had a terminal case of cancer. His first reaction was one of shock and disbelief. On being reassured, he began to wonder how he would cope with the issue, how he would act now toward his father, what he would be able to do for his mother and sister throughout the time of crisis, whether he would be strong enough to accomplish what was expected of him until the day his father was buried. He felt too small, too weak, too helpless to bear up under such a trying situation. But then just as he was experiencing his insufficiency, as he describes it, he seemed to "grow." He perceived himself as being at the same time both large and small. He was somehow convinced that he would be big enough to handle the problem. He was reassured by this feeling, and actually was a great help to both his father and the rest of the family in their time of need. This was a peak experience for the seminarian, because from it he learned something lasting both about the problem of death and about himself.

A priest relates a similar experience about "splitting" when he heard the news about the murder of Dr. Martin Luther King. As he was driving home the bulletin came over the car radio. The shock of the report made him feel strange and eerie, not like himself at all. He seemed almost to be like someone else, someone far away, and yet he knew he was indeed himself, because he was able to continue to drive his car and arrive safely home.

This experience of the double-self has been studied by a number of psychologists, notably by Otto Rank. Its origins might be sought, according to Rank, in a personal fear of death. Rank relates it to ordinary phenomena like one's shadow, the image of oneself in a mirror, and the self in dreams. He sees here the bases for forming the notion of a "self outside of one's self." The phantasy of a person under the influence of a desire to escape death proposes the double as an insurance against extinction. The double becomes the symbol of the psyche's energetic denial of the power of death. From the notion of the double, Rank thinks, the idea of an immortal soul evolved. The soul was first perceived as a double of the body, but unlike the body it was considered to be indestructible. As such it achieved a certain religious significance among the peoples of the ancient world. The Egyptians were found to be particularly sensitive to this notion. They proposed two souls, the *ba* or life principle, and the *ka* or double-image, which was often represented by a statue or clay model of the person. From the eighteenth dynasty on mummies were placed in coffins shaped like a human being. The sculptured faces resembled the features of the deceased. Thus was the *ka* preserved. In Egyptian literature as well as in the legends of other ancient peoples there often occurs a story of two brothers who looked alike, but were quite different temperamentally. Undoubtedly here again we encounter the double prototype in a different form.

In witchcraft and voodoo a little doll-like image of a person to be hexed is fashioned out of clay. A needle or other sharp instrument is thrust into it; maybe its head will be knocked off; the practitioner expects that through the power of his magic a similar tragedy will strike the person whose double it is. Even highly sophisticated society tries to preserve the memory of its heroes or notables by enshrining their likeness in marble or oil.

The psychic device of the double-self is another modality of expression for the phenomenon of the union of opposites which is quite typical in many kinds of peak experiences. These two different selves harbor the contrary or contradictory elements; yet the two selves really form one and the same person. Thus in the logic of the ancients the body is material and mortal; its double the soul is immaterial and immortal. The union of the two makes the complete individual. In the phenomenon of the double-self the fully conscious is reconciled with what lies in the dark area beyond the terminator of consciousness.

Analyses of the phenomenon of transcendence in peak experiences tend to reveal that it occurs very often not in the field of high conscious concentration, but in some other more hidden area of the psyche. This fact possibly accounts for some of the experiences, like that of the double-self, associated with the perception of a reconciliation of opposites in states of high psychic tension. The breakthrough, the transcendence, comes as a kind of surprise. By a sort of "serendipity," or happy accident, one finds that he can be basically at peace even while angry or frustrated, or big and strong even while feeling small and weak. Nor can he trace the cause of this experience. It is radically paradoxical, and defies any full explanation. Out of the dark area of consciousness there suddenly looms large and bright just the opposite of what one is highly conscious of.

Dr. Paul Gordon, a professor at Chicago Medical School, must have had a peak experience of a scientific sort when he discovered what seems to be the first non-toxic, wide-spectrum anti-viral agent, isoprinosine. Yet he was not working in the field of virus research at all. He was looking for a drug that would heighten memory responses and facilitate learning. Noting the possibilities of the agent in this area, he was surprised to discover its additional value in interfering with viral action by blocking the transfer of genetic information from viruses to their host cells. The breakthrough was the result of sheer serendipity!

A cognate phenomenon often occurs in sleep. Here the dream often brings about a reconciliation between a state of psychic tension and the surcease from it that sleep is. Freud looked upon dreams as vehicles of wish fulfillment. The agitated person, when he goes to bed, wishes to be freed from his anxiety, and the dreams that he has often symbolize that wish, and, indeed, prevent his problems from intruding into the state of peace he has attained in sleep. Sometimes a reversal of this process will take place. A person is very tired and goes to bed. During the night there is a disturbance in the neighborhood. The house across the street catches fire, and the silence of the night is transformed into a cacophony of sirens, roaring motors, gushing streams of water and yelling voices. This bedlam, of course, does register in some way on the hearing apparatus of the sleeper. The sounds are loud enough to rouse him from his deep sleep. But he begins to dream that he is a fireman involved in fighting a great conflagration. The sounds that he hears become a part of his dream. So he is able to reconcile in the double of himself that the dream provides the opposite impression of needing quiet rest and being stirred by the excitement of what is happening outside.

One of the most common experiences of the phenomenon of transcendence in the reconciliation of opposites occurs in the transformation of a fear or horror of an object into a desire or fascination for it. A most commonly encountered fear is inspired by snakes. Everyone has heard a story like the one told by a young lady. She had a terrible dread of all crawling and creeping animals. She spent a summer vacation period at a dude ranch out west. While riding through the desert country she was suddenly thrown from her balking horse and landed a scant four feet away from an irritated rattler sounding his eerie warning. She was paralyzed not so much with fear as with a fascination for the ominous reptile. In her eyes it was this fascination that prevented her from panicking and forestalled the deadly strike until she could be rescued from her predicament. Very often the fear of what is reported to exist in a haunted house is perceived as the ultimate motive that drives little boys to explore it with great fascination. What makes a game of Russian roulette intriguing and tantalizing may very well be an intense fear of death.

The seminarian who worked as an orderly in a hospital and on the occasion of the death of the patient he was tending experienced a transformation of his anger and frustration into peace and contentment felt that this peak experience had a further influence on his whole life. His reflections revealed to him that before the incident he had a great horror and dread of death. As a result of this experience he believed that he was able to transcend this attitude. Indeed, his fear was not precisely tranformed into desire, but into an acceptance of death and a new appreciation of it as something that could be meaningful and even beautiful.

A student related that from his childhood he always had a dread of being caught on a railroad crossing as a fast train approached. Often he would dream that his foot was snagged in the boards placed over the tracks on the pedestrian walk. He would be startled into full consciousness just as the train was about to smash into him. One day in later life, when his car stalled on a railroad track, as the crossing gates lowered in front and back of him, he felt a strange fascination which slowed his efforts to start the motor of his car and drive around the gates.

A common characteristic of these peak experiences that involve some kind of union of opposites is the fact that they are thematized in later reflection around ultimate issues. Most frequently the question revolves about life or death. But other pivotal issues are also encountered. Sometimes, as in the case of splitting, or of the double, the alternative is between the self and non-self. In other experiences one is forced, as it were, to choose between belief and disbelief; in still others between meaningfulness and absurdity. But the resolution of the problem is invariably seen to lie in the avoidance of the dilemma. It is not a question of either-or, but of both-and. One is reminded of the solution that Jesus gave to the problem of the coin of tribute posed by the Pharisees.

Of particular interest to a study of religious experience is the issue of meaningfulness and absurdity. The avoidance of an absurd position was one of the chief factors in the logical argument for the existence of God from a perception of order in the universe. It is absurd to think that order proceeds from chaos; it has to result from intelligence. But the modern atheist can argue logically in similar fashion. There is great waste in the universe. In almost every quarter of human experience evidence is given of massive dysteleology. It is absurd to think that such a chaotic condition is the effect of an intelligent and benevolent God.

The meaninglessness of man's own best efforts is a favorite theme of Jean-Paul Sartre. In a poignant short story entitled *The Wall* he points up the absurdity of human intention in a rather facetious way. Pablo, the hero (or anti-hero), is a loyalist captured by *falangistas* during the Spanish civil war. He is imprisoned with several others in the cellar of an old hospital. He fears that he will have to undergo the same fate suffered by so many of his captured loyalist comrades. His hands will be tied, his eyes blindfolded, and his body pushed against a wall. A volley will ring out, and he will be dead. He is paralyzed with fear at the thought of it. He asks a doctor imprisoned with him how it will feel when the bullets crash into his body. Suppose they hit no vital organ. Suppose he has to lie writhing in pain while the squad reloads and fires again. He feels that the only reason he has been kept alive is that the fascists suspect that he knows the whereabouts of a certain important leader of the loyalist movement.

Pablo knows that eventually he will be executed, but he resolves that before he dies he will play one last trick on his enemies. In his view the *falangistas* are all martinets. If they thought they knew where the important loyalist leader was hiding, there would be a flurry of military activity. Orders would ring out; trucks would be summoned; arms would be inspected; the search party would scurry off in great haste and with a great display of military precision. And it would be all for nothing! Pablo knew he would die, but at least the last laugh would be his.

When summoned for questioning he played the game for a while. He said he did not know the whereabouts of his friend. He maintained that he was not able to reveal it even if he was tortured. It was a good show to the final act when he broke down and admitted that the man the fascists wanted was hiding in a well-known cemetery, perhaps, as he said, in one of the vaults or in the grave-digger's shack. It was, of course, the one place he was sure his friend would avoid.

Pablo waited and tried to picture the grim fascists with their pert moustaches methodically searching the cemetery, lifting up tombstones and opening the doors of vaults in precise order. He felt a macabre sort of gaiety. Upon return of the

search party he knew that orders for his immediate execution
would be issued. But it did not come to pass. Instead, he was
for the first time given the freedom of the courtyard outside
the hospital. He was even allowed to take his meal in the mess
with the other prisoners. In the evening some new prisoners
arrived, and one of them told Pablo that the *falangistas* got
his friend. They found him in the grave-digger's shack in the
cemetery and shot him.

Existentialists like Jean-Paul Sartre contend that all life
is absurd and meaningless; logic can do nothing but compound
the difficulty. The very means they use to illustrate the absurdity of existence must, however, be meaningful. If the story of
The Wall were totally meaningless, if it struck no chord of
recognition in human experience, it would not have become the
significant piece of literature that it is. Rather than prove the
contention of the author, the story points to the possibility in
experience of reconciling opposites. It illustrates the meaningfulness of meaninglessness. And in so doing it might attain a
place in the *genre* of religious experiential literature like the
New Testament itself, which inculcates the meaningfulness
of the meaninglessness of the cross.

Karl Jaspers has remarked: "When I am completely myself, I am no longer only myself." The law of union of opposites in peak experience is also evidenced in the relatively
frequent phenomenon of subject-object identity. The consciousness of adults in highly civilized societies character-
istically enjoys the faculty to discriminate easily between what
is subjective and what is objective in experience. Apart from
scientific and technical questions, as for instance whether color
is really in the object or in the eye, the knower realizes full
well that he is not identified with what he is considering. Even
when he turns his gaze to some part of his own body, for
example, his foot, he is aware of its being simultaneously a
segment of himself and an object of his awareness. The French
philosopher Descartes highlighted in his epistemology this
dichotomy between subject and object. But recent psycho-

logical studies have indicated that such a distinction is not as sharply made in infants, and even in adults in more primitive cultures. The loss of this discriminatory power between the subjective and objective is experienced also when certain drugs like LSD are employed. This loss provides one of the truly fascinating aspects of the psychedelic trip.

A lessening of this discriminatory power can be noted in subjects who continuously use a tool in their work. After a while the tool, as it were, becomes a part of themselves, an extension of their own hand as far as their mind and judgment are concerned. The same can be said for dentures or other prostheses. Cab drivers and others who use cars habitually come in their non-reflective states to regard their autos in the same light: not as an object, but as an extension of their own being. The increasing use of group techniques in business and administrative operations is tending to produce in our time a new kind of consciousness in which the group is comprehended as another, wider, more extended self. While one might be quite Apollonian in his private life, he inclines toward the assumption of a new Dionysian consciousness in a group. So he views others associated with him not as mere objects of his consciousness, but together with himself as a kind of organism with its own distinctive consciousness in which he shares.

The technique of "no-mind" in Zen has long been seen as a vehicle to facilitate the breakdown of the subject-object dichotomy in individual consciousness with consequent experience of *satori,* or enlightenment. Eventually the disciple of this way will see himself as one with everything he experiences. While walking in the woods the student of Zen may experience the sky, the earth, the trees, the flowers, the pools and streams, in short everything he encounters, as in reality identified with himself. He will be able to exclaim that he has ceased to be himself, that he has become the trees and flowers as well!

But when the contrast between an habitual state of sharp discrimination between subject and object and a sudden and unusual experience of its loss strikes the consciousness, one will often describe what he feels as a peak experience. Thus a student told how he was walking down a road in a wooded area on the shore of a lake. It was night, and the stars were shining brightly. All of a sudden he felt as if he were not alone. He was aware of a presence that overwhelmed him. He felt as if he were a part of all that he was experiencing, or as if it were a part of him. His own being seemed to extend into the outer reaches of space. He was identified with the water, the trees, the air, the stars. This was for him a peak experience, and he interpreted it as an experience of God.

Another type of peak experience of subject-object identity has definite psychological and theological implications. Many people identify their entry into a particular organization like a church as a peak experience. Some look to their graduation as a lawyer or doctor or their enlistment into the military service as a turning point in their lives. Still others view their marriage or ordination as the most significant thing that ever happened to them.

It is possible to classify this kind of experience as a transcendence achieved through a form of subject-object identification.

A teacher pointed out that one of his peak experiences was undoubtedly an intrauterine one. As a child he reflected often on the feeling of being alive that he remembered as his first sensation. This experience was, of course, highly undifferentiated. It was basically an experience of the contrast between nothingness and what he later realized as life. Here indeed there could be no subject-object discrimination. In this experience and the reflections upon it in childhood what was perceived was life itself, life unlocated and undirected.

Some psychologists have interpreted the function of organizations in the life of an individual in terms of a another-symbol, a maternal surrogate. Primitive peoples, as especially those in Polynesia, often have a lodge or large house for the exclusive use of males in the community. All the males who have been initiated into the village brotherhood through a

special puberty-ritual have free and open access to this house;
all other persons by a strict law of taboo are enjoined from
entering it. When at puberty a young boy separates himself
forever from his mother, at an initiation ritual he is led to a
new womb. The rite celebrates and satisfies his wish for re-
gression to an infantile state of existence; but he would never
dare express this wish to be still attached to his mother in any
other way than through this ceremony. For it would be perceived by all as unmanly. The house of males after his initiation becomes for him a new permanent womb, a mother-surro-
gate, that is completely acceptable and commendable in terms
of the culture in which he lives. Here he can forget the worries
and cares of his manly estate, and enjoy the pleasure of just
existing and feeling accepted. Here as in the uterus one is free
of all responsibility. By identifying himself with the male
house and his tribal brothers in it, the young man has for a
while exonerated himself of the burdens of adulthood, and re-
gressed to a more placid and secure state of existence. He has
lost himself once again in the womb.

In highly civilized areas the same phenomenon may also
occur, although the relationship of the "gang" or "club" to the
womb may be buried deeper down in the dark area of consciousness. But it does pop up now and again even in our
language. When a young man goes off to school, the *alma
mater* provides him with a surrogate womb. If he goes off to
sea, he will refer to his ship as "she." If he swears the blood
oath of the *mafioso* he will call the brotherhood *la santa mama*.

But it is especially in the Church that this kind of subject-
object identification becomes fully feasible through faith.

When Jesus was informed by one of his listeners that his
mother and his brothers were in the area looking for him, how
did he respond? He pointed to his new brotherhood, to those
who were associated with him in his work, and replied: "Here
are my *mother* and my brothers!" (Mt. 12: 46ff). The community that considered him its founder was from its earliest
days looked upon as a mother to all who would become Jesus'

brothers through the rite of initiation. It was holy Mother Church. In the womb of that Church, in the baptismal font, every believer could fully identify his own selfhood, his own subjectivity, with the very object of his faith, the Lord Jesus himself! By symbolically dying and rising with him the baptized became one with him. Were it completely understood and appreciated by the initiate, this would be the peak of all of his experiences. No more transcending subject-object identification could ever be possible for man.

The law of union of opposites, which in some way must be operative in every peak experience, is certainly its most significant characteristic. The second identifying note, however, is the one, I dare say, which most people employ to identify certain of their experiences as peak. It is the deep impression that such an experience makes: the lasting character of such a happening. Not that the moment of perception itself lasts for any notable length of time; the greatest experiences may be ones that occupied only a few seconds; but the experience is perceived to be permanent and enduring in its consequences upon life, in the changes that have resulted from it. People who have had peak experiences will always point out that they have profoundly metamorphosized their life-style, or at least their view of life. The peak experience gives one a brand new view of self. One comes to realize that there is a broader horizon than was hitherto suspected in his own possibility of transcendence. What he has experienced may well be categorized as a kind of personal miracle. He has been made aware in a practical and realistic way of the dark side of his consciousness. He has enjoyed an exposure to new, and perhaps undreamed of, personal resources. Every peak experience is indeed a fuller revelation of self; but it may also be, in a sense, a revelation of what lies beyond the self.

The third characteristic of peak experience is that it contains some element of mystery. What is experienced is strange to the subject. He is so unaccustomed to it that he finds that the ordinary means of identification often break down. The insight that accompanies an ordinary experience, where mental symbols really fit and categorize the object one is experiencing, sets the mind at rest, and brings about a subjective state of self-reassurance. But that insight is often lacking in peak experience. What is sensed is highly ambiguous. It has a certain ill-defined quality about it. This may engender a response in the affectivity which tends to reinforce the apprehension. The concealed and unfamiliar element in the experience may arouse a feeling of uncanniness. It may stimulate sheer dread and creeping horror. Or, on the other hand, it may produce fascination and delight. What is experienced may be perceived as unusually beautiful, attractive and sublime.

The ambiguity of the perception may be produced by a heightened awareness of the limitations of sensation, judgment or consciousness itself. One may not be able to perceive whether what he is experiencing is alive or lifeless. He may not be able to tell whether the personal influence or presence he senses is human or not. Or, on the other hand, the ambiguity may result from a surprising extension of conscious activity. This usually occurs when there suddenly appears in experience a coincidence of hitherto totally unrelated data. In either case, at least indirectly attention is called to the terminator of consciousness and its operation in the experience.

In conjunction with this third characteristic of peak experiences there often occurs a fourth which may be described as hyper- or hypo-aesthesia. The activity of the sensorium may be heightened so that one perceives data which ordinarily lie beyond the limen of consciousness. Or, conversely, the activity of certain psychic operators may be dulled or suspended so that one has the eerie feeling that he should be sensing something he is not.

Our era is witness to a rebellion against reason. The pendulum is swinging away from the highly rationalistic structures of the past. The power of reasoning is no longer exclusively man's thing. Computers are able to outstrip the human mind in calculating and guiding. Our era is protesting

against this terrible affront to human dignity. It is beginning
more and more to cultivate the alogical, the non-rational,
aspects of human existence. The absurd, the highly emotional,
the psychedelic, the occult and inexplicable occupy the attention of all, particularly of young people, more than ever today.
In religious activity too a new slant on faith is emerging. Emphasis is shifting from the *parousia* to the *kenosis*. Faith is no
longer viewed so much as a link with the invisible, but ever-
present God. It is beginning more and more to be apprehended
as the awesome responsibility of carrying out God's work in a
world that God has abandoned. As Bonhoeffer put it, the God
who is really with us is the God who has left us on our own.
Connected with this concept is the notion of Hegel that Jesus
is really the kenotic Word, pure negativity, which makes void
all that is old and worn to become the source of all new life
and activity.

The fifth characteristic of the peak experience is that it
is alogical. Indeed it creates a logical vacuum which, although
defying explanation, very often leads to a new and better
integrated view of life. Not only is there always an aura of
mystery about peak experience—and this would be a challenge
to the mind—but in it the sensorium and affectivity, and not
the intellect, predominate. Thus the peak experience reverses
the situation that normally holds sway in consciousness. In
ordinary experience sensation and affectivity lie outside the
main focus of awareness. The major conscious effort is ex-
pended on thought processes, on ideas, evaluations and judgments. But a peak experience may be truly one of the kenotic
word, that is, one which defies comprehension, logic, judgment,
evaluation and expression. It can only be described as truly ineffable. Other psychic elements crowd out of the center of
awareness the normal mental reactions: they are relegated to
an unaccustomed position closer to the terminator of consciousness. And hence even reflection on this kind of experience is
rendered more difficult because the normal mnemonic guidance
cues like order and meaning are either lacking or not fully

developed. The peak experience, then, unlike ordinary experience, usually becomes a meaningful structure to the psyche only in reflection, when the mind once again can assume its wonted place in the limelight of awareness. But, of course, the total experience cannot be fully recreated in reflection. Only those data which made some impact upon the logical structure of the ego will be the ones most likely to be recalled.

A sixth characteristic of the peak experience is that it seems to be more a passive than an active one. The subject apprehends himself as acted upon. He is gripped and led by a power over which he has no direct control. He finds here one source of his feeling of helplessness or frustration. This power he senses is not always projected as coming from without; sometimes it seems to well up from within the psyche. When the dynamic of the experience revolves about the apprehension of subject-object identification, the active power is likely to be viewed as coming from without, but in the case of the self versus the non-self perception it may be judged to emanate from within.

The uncontrollable quality of a peak experience has been the object of some study. Is it merely an illusion? Is the real reason that the experience cannot be readily terminated or dismissed the fact that it is so fascinating, so gripping, so alluring that the subject does not really want to let loose of it? Or is it so enervating that the subject lacks the ability to muster the psychic energy to force it out of the field of awareness? Or is it the fact that activities of the mind and will are pushed out of the focus of attention and the alogical elements of the psyche take over the reason for the subject's perceived inability to control this kind of experience? Or is there actually some power outside the subject that obsesses him and prevents any exercise of control? Science today is not in a position to give an apodictic answer to these questions, or to marshal proofs to substantiate any one of the possible theories they may suggest. We simply have to say that we do not know for certain. And indeed in different cases one or several of these explanations may be validated by the data of experience itself.

People who have peak experiences will generally report that they just happened; they were not consciously produced. Most would be of the opinion that in this area of psychic phenomenology there can be no such thing as a command performance. Just by willing it one cannot have such an experience. And this is the reason why they would interpret it as principally a passive experience. But studies of oriental mysticism seem to warrant the conclusion that what might be considered a peak experience, at least in the western world, can be produced by the use of a number of simple techniques. The Zen Buddhist tyro begins his training with the conviction that he will eventually be able to have an experience of *satori*. The old master may live continually in such an experience. It would seem that where peak experiences are relatively rare, where there is no cultivation of the psychic techniques which might facilitate them, or where the onset of them is gradual and insidious (as we mentioned before) and not sudden and unmistakable, the persuasion that they are not actively produced by the psyche is rife. But where this kind of experience is more highly esteemed as a part of life itself, where it seemingly occurs with greater frequency, and is taken more for granted, there one encounters the conviction that this kind of experience can be forthcoming if and when a person desires it, provided only he knows how to conjure it up. This is not to say that in the estimation of the oriental mystics there is no power greater than the psyche involved in the process. They would only seem to indicate that whatever is needed to produce this kind of experience, from within the psyche as well as from without, is at hand if one knows what to do.

The seventh and last characteristic of the peak experience that we shall present is one that, as the reader will undoubtedly perceive, underlies all of the observations we have made thus far about this type of phenomenon. It is also one, as we shall shortly see, that is most important and significant in the interpretation of religious experience. A peak experience is basically always ambivalent. This means not only that it is mysterious, obscure and ambiguous, as we have already seen. It means precisely that it is open to a number of different interpretations and susceptible to a plurality of evaluations. Since it comprises a union of opposites one might have suspected right from the beginning of our discourse that this is so. Since it relates to phenomena that lie along the terminator of consciousness, or at least not in the focal position of attention, since, in other words, it is basically an ambiguous experience, one might have concluded that then it must also be ambivalent. We have also said that since the peak experience is principally alogical, it is hardly self-explanatory. Interpretation and evaluation can be rendered only in a reflection. And for this, at any one given time, only certain elements of the original experience can be recalled. And various aspects can give rise to different interpretations.

So the subject of the experience sometimes finds himself in the difficult position of having to answer both yes and no to questions posed about it. Was it a perception of something actual, some physical reality outside? Or was it a purely psychic phenomenon, produced wholly from within? Did it seem to be the kind of experience any normal person could have? Or was it strange and abnormal? Was it something supernatural? Or was it just a natural psychic phenomenon? Could it have been an experience of God? Or just of one's denied self?

4

THE EXPERIENCE OF GOD

From what has preceded the reader will see that there are two basic issues to be handled when we address ourselves to the consideration of the one type of peak experience that we are especially interested in, the experience of God or his grace. The first question is practical and pastoral. How do I recognize an experience of God? What are its parameters? The second question is theological. Can an experience of God lead to an affirmation of God as a reality? What would be the dynamics of such a process?

Scripture gives us many models of theophanies and of experiences of God. One that is most familiar and useful, since it would fall clearly into the category of peak experience is that of the transfiguration of Christ. According to the version in Luke (9: 28-36) while Jesus was praying on a mountain, his face was transformed, and his garments became radiant. Suddenly Moses and Elijah appeared and engaged in conversation with him. While Jesus was praying, the apostles he had taken with him, Peter, John and James, had fallen asleep. But suddenly they awoke and beheld the scene. Peter expressed his delight by saying: "Master, how good it is for us to be here! Let's put up three tents, one for you, one for Moses, and one for Elijah!" The evangelist notes that he really did not know what he was saying. At this point a cloud overshadowed them, and they became fearful. A voice from the cloud proclaimed: "This is my Son, my chosen One. Listen to him." Suddenly the vision ended, and Jesus was alone with his apostles, who told no one at the time about the experience they had had.

This incident exemplifies very well the characteristics of an experience of God. It has to be described, first of all, as numinous. That is, it is endowed with other-worldly qualities. The face of Jesus and his garments are changed; there is a strange radiance about them. Persons from the world beyond the grave, Moses and Elijah, have their place in the experience.

Secondly, the experience is nebulous. There are many obscure, unclear elements. The participants are for a time enveloped in a cloud. From this cloud a mysterious voice sounds, elucidating the purpose of the divine visitation.

Thirdly, it is mystic. The chiaro-oscuro setting reveals as much as it conceals. It leaves to the imagination the task of picturing the awesome presence in the cloud, whose brilliance is only reflected in what is actually seen. It appeals to the mysterious, deep, unexplored elements of the human psyche. It excites feelings that best correspond with what lies on the dark side of the terminator of consciousness.

Fourthly, the experience is symbolic. Some of the concrete elements of the vision have by tradition acquired a well-known, significant, religious meaning. Symbols link the past to the present and future. A symbol is a sign standing for the thing it represents. A sign is some person or thing which, when perceived, leads to the knowledge of something other than itself. There are natural signs and conventional signs. Natural signs may be images, as for instance, a statue or picture of a person from which one gets a good deal of information about the person himself. Other natural signs are not images, but still impart some knowledge about things distinct from themselves. Thus, for instance, smoke is a natural sign of combustion. Arbitrary or conventional signs are those which are established by public authority or common human usage. Thus the flag of the United States is a sign of our government, and the ampersand the sign of a copulative conjunction in writing. When, however, the flag is saluted and honored, it takes the place of the thing it represents. It then becomes a symbol. It is cathected with the significance that is attached primarily to the thing it signifies: the American way of life, our form of government, the people of this country, the principles of freedom upon which our constitution rests, etc.

In the history of the Jewish people Moses was the lawgiver. Elijah was one of the major prophets. In the vision on the mountain these figures become symbols of the two mainstays of Jewish religious belief, the law and the prophets. They point to Jesus as the fulfillment of the law and the realization of prophecy.

The cloud too plays a symbolic role. For the Jew it was a sign of mysterious power. He was not able to see how it could remain suspended between heaven and earth. He welcomed the beneficial effects of the rain that fell from it upon his land, but stood in awe at its destructive force, such as was unleashed at the time of the deluge. During their journey in the desert for forty years Yahweh led his people during the day through the instrumentality of a cloud. In the vision on the mountain the cloud could be interpreted as a symbol of Yahweh himself, now prepared to lead his people to the true passover, of which the former was only a sign, in the paschal mystery of Jesus.

In the vision Jesus himself can also be apprehended as a symbol, for the rays of glory that shone in him might have been interpreted as portentious signs presaging in the minds of believers his eschatological role.

Fifthly, the experience of the apostles is obviously ecstatic. It is rapturous. In the experience the disciples were really not themselves. They were transported outside themselves. In the transcendence that is achieved in this kind of experience one is apt to say things that might appear to be strange and foolish. Thus the evangelist indicates that when Peter made his offer to memorialize the incident, he really did not know what he was saying. He was rapt out of his senses. His was obviously an experience of pure delight and fascination. So he wanted it to continue, to perdure always as it was, for his offer was to build dwellings for Jesus and his visitors from the other world. At the very least he seems to want, if

the experience could not continue, to have something to mark
it in his memory forever, so that he could on occasion live in
the recollection of it by visiting the place where it had occurred.

Sixthly, the experience is liminal. That is, it skirts the
borderline between the world of dreams and fancy and the
world of reality. It is basically open to interpretation as something actual though numinous, or a fantasy produced by an
illusory or hallucinogenic operation of the psyche. Obviously
the intent of the text is to minimize the possibility of con-
cluding that the experience could have been an illusion. The
fact that there were three witnesses practically excludes any
type of psychic aberration; it would leave open only the possibility of mass hypnotism. But in all honesty, the evangelist
notes the fact that the three apostles had been sleeping. This
admission points up both the fact that at the time of the experience they were not sleeping, and the likelihood that they
had not yet reached the condition of full and perfect alertness
that would characterize the awareness of one who had been
fully awake for some time. Thus the liminal situation which
occurs in so many religious experiences may at least be implied
in this one by the gospel text itself.

The seventh and final characteristic of this experience that
we shall consider is its ineffability. The apostles did not speak
about what happened at least at the moment. People who have
had peak religious experiences often report that they are not
really able to tell what happened to them. The sheer awesome-
ness and indescribability of what they witnessed mutes them.
Only after considerable reflection, after the subject can assign
some meaning and significance to what he experienced, will
he be able to relate it to others. Indeed, when he has apprehended the full significance of what happened to him, the subject very often feels compelled to share his experience with
someone. Eventually, after much reflection and integration of
their experience with other memories of Jesus, Peter, James

and John became witnesses of the fact that they had come into contact with God himself in this mountain episode. Their experience was one of God; to this they gave testimony.

Undoubtedly the evangelists who reported this incident intended to consider it in their testimony as an historical fact. But, of course, a distinction has to be made between the subjective experience and the object of the experience. If the experience itself was an historical fact, we still have no guarantee or no way of finding out if what was seen was objectively verifiable, was itself historical. Were the data of the vision produced only in the consciousness of those present, or could they also have been detected by photographic instrumentation like light meters and cameras? To be considered historical one today might well require that they be objectively verifiable. But in either case, whether we consider the incident to have been an historical or purely subjective phenomenon, one fact seems certain from the testimony of those involved. They understand it to have been a divinely produced experience.

Scripture provides many other instances of similar kinds of peak religious experience. Interest focusses today particularly on the numerous appearances of Jesus after his resurrection where once again the question of historicity is raised. These appearances exhibit many or all of the characteristics we have observed to have been operative in the incident of the transfiguration. But here the evangelists show themselves to be more concerned with an objective verification of the data. Jesus' risen body was perceived as an other-worldly one that could pass through doors; yet it could still be felt and fed; and it bore the identifying marks of the crucifixion. There was indeed something strange and mysterious about that risen body. Jesus was not immediately recognized even by those who had been very close to him. His apostles had their doubts; yet they did not dare ask if it were really he. Only Thomas was brash enough to do this in a rather indirect way. Ultimately only their faith in him and his word assured the followers of

Jesus that he had indeed arisen. Historical facts like the empty tomb were at best only indications that helped support the insight of faith.

The characteristics we have considered in this biblical example of an experience of God appear also most frequently in other instances. They serve well as basic criteria for the pastor to use in assisting his clients to come to some judgment about their peak religious experience.

When confronted with a report of unusual religious phenomena, of course, the first thing the pastor must do is to ascertain the basic psychological condition of the subject. Peter, James and John are not portrayed in the gospel as psychotic or neurotic. They are simple, hard-working fishermen who enjoy soundness of both mind and body. We have already stated that the causes of hallucinations and illusions are ordinarily readily identifiable. We have listed these causes, and fuller descriptions of them are available in handbooks of pastoral theology or manuals of psychology. Besides, the pastor's own personal knowledge of the individual involved will ultimately be the best criterion he can have for the preliminary judgment he must make.

Once he has evaluated the basic soundness of the person who reports unusual religious experiences, the minister will find it helpful to use the characteristic notes of a divine visitation that have been set forth. It would, however, be a grave error to allow a judgment to be made on the basis of these alone. As we have seen, every peak experience, religious or not, is fundamentally ambivalent. There is always a powerful temptation to resolve this ambivalence on the basis of a personal philosophy or mind-set or a handy list of criteria. And, of course, it cannot be resolved in this way at all. To be sure, as a genuine part of the experience itself, the ambivalence has to be allowed to stand; to tamper with it would be to mutilate an essential element in the report of the client.

We can now announce the first central thesis of our essay.

If God does appear in human experience, in so doing he can neither violate his own being nor the characteristic operation of the consciousness of his human host.

That which is totally other to man normally must make its presence felt on the terminator of consciousness. The adage of scripture that no man ever saw God and lived must guide our reasoning in this matter. God does not appear in a formally recognizable way in the focus of human awareness. To be perceived he must be objectified. But as object he cannot be like any that are familiar, any to which some meaning has already been attached. Nor can these be used with full effectiveness as bearings or reference points either to locate God in experience or provide definite analogs for the attachment of meaning to the objectification of God in consciousness. God even as the objectified must stand in human awareness as an absolutely unique, nonpareil, incomprehensible, non-referable reality. Consequently he must stand on the terminator of consciousness. To focalize him would be to lose him as an object of awareness. The only contact point in the consciousness that can correspond to the unlimited being of God is the terminator which appears as the threshold of the limitless void or expanse that is projected to lie beyond. But what stands on the terminator of consciousness is necessarily ambiguous, and gives rise to ambivalence. Ambivalence, then, far from being a deterrent to the affirmation of God's presence in an experience, is a *sine qua non* of such an apprehension. As we have said, St. Augustine long ago remarked that if what you conceive is certainly God, then what you conceive certainly is not God. The same formula must be applied, *mutatis mutandis,* to the perception of God in experience.

In their reflections upon a religious experience both the pastor and his client must as far as possible purge their considerations of any preset convictions or philosophies of interpretation. If one has had an experience of God, God and not the subject, has produced it, and only God can authenticate it in the insight of the client. Generalizations are precarious when one deals with experience unless they emanate from the carefully controlled situation of the psychological laboratory. As we said, there really can be no verification of experience from without. The role of the pastor in this situation is not one of judge or authenticator, but of facilitator only. But he cannot facilitate by allowing his own opinions or wishes to cloud the reflections of his client.

A seminarian had had a peak experience which deeply affected his attitude on death and the meaning of life. While he had no problem in accepting this as a religious experience in the widest sense of the term, he did not see it as resulting in any way from a direct intervention of God. In a group of people who were relating some of their peak experiences, the seminarian was quite agitated because one or other of the participants identified their experiences clearly and cogently as encounters with God. He kept vexing them by asking repeatedly how they knew it really was God. When the seminarian told of his experience a couple of others tried to bring him to the point where he would reinterpret it as an experience of God. He became more angry and frustrated, and pointed out how he resented their trying to tailor what he experienced to fit their own needs. But what he did not see immediately was that he was trying to accomplish in regard to their experience the very same thing he accused them of doing in regard to his own. He was trying to interpret their experiences of an encounter with God in the light of his own peak experience, and so eliminate any reference to God; and they were trying to interpret his experience in the light of their own, and so to insert the element they considered most significant, the reference to God. Later on the seminarian told how he learned from this incident that the only possible stance of a minister in circumstances like these is one of basic and unrelenting openness.

Students of scholastic theology, and in particular those of the Thomistic school, will remember a very important book published by Antonin Massoulié, who died early in the eighteenth century. It was entitled *Divus Thomas sui interpres de divina motione et libertate creata,* and as the title suggests it set forth the simple notion that, amid all the arguments and disputes that were rampant at that time, particularly between the Dominicans and Jesuits, as to how the doctrine of St. Thomas on the question of freedom and predestination was to be understood, St. Thomas himself, after all, was the best interpreter of his own doctrine. So Massoulié proceeded by comparing Thomistic text with Thomistic text to try to arrive at a clear understanding of the doctrine.

The second central point of this essay is that this principle ought also to be followed in the case of the experience of God. The person who has had the experience is the best interpreter of his own experience. No pastor, no outsider, no close friend even, is in any position whatsoever to interpret authentically the experience of another. The only real interpretation possible must come from the person who had the experience. If he says that he did not have an experience of God, no one else can say that it was. If he states that he experienced God, by what right can anyone deny it? As we stated before, no one can have or even fully appreciate the experience of another. The only equitable attitude that a minister can assume in a situation like this is one of openness and basic trust, provided that he knows his client to be generally stable and reliable. It is only from such a vantage point that he will really be able to be of assistance.

Any interpretation of peak experience, as we have stated, will take place in a reflection distinct from and following after the experience itself. Since this is the case, one always runs some risk that the subject will not himself interpret his experience principally from within. That is, the intellectual attitudes and propensities, or even the downright prejudices, of the subject may obscure the data of the experience and distort the judgment that is pronounced upon it. This is true, and is one of the risks that has to be taken by the minister, although in an interview he can generally discover prejudicial stances of his client.

If an experience in reality has God for its author, if it is in fact God-given, belief in it as such is attained formally in a reflective act that follows. But this belief has definitely to be referred to the experience itself, and cannot be related primarily to the general religious attitudes or philosophy of the subject. The foundation of this particular belief has to be perceived as located in the dark area of experience that lies beyond the terminator of consciousness. Thus in the scriptural example we have used, it is the voice from the cloud that grounds the apostles' persuasion that this experience was a real theophany — not precisely their general faith in Jesus as an emissary from God. The chiaro-oscuro fabric of this ground of their belief must have been focussed in a subsequent reflection. Their remembering of similar incidents in the history of their people when God had spoken and acted from a cloud was for them a triggering device, an interpretative guide, for their belief, but not precisely the motive.

The third central thesis of this essay is that the final and decisive, the very best, interpreter of a peak experience, if indeed it be an experience of God, is the one who gives the experience. Even the interpretation of the one who has the experience must yield to the interpretation of the one who produces it. At times the awareness of God in such an experience can seem most pivotal and compelling. From out of the obscure area beyond the terminator of consciousness emanates an influence like that experienced in post-hypnotic suggestion. This power ineluctably draws the subject to accept his experience as an encounter with God.

On the other hand, the complete absence of any concrete referent to God in his experience will rightly lead the subject to conclude from his reflection that he has had no divine visitation. Though the experience he had was significant and has perhaps to be integrated with his life of faith since it will make a notable difference in his attitudes and behavior, it was not precisely a religious experience. He had a peak experience, and that is all.

We have been describing clear-cut incidents where the subject is able to identify whether his experience is one of God or not. But many people report borderline cases which they are not able to decide. The subject cannot place himself in either category of certainty; he is in doubt. He can recollect no experiential contact with what lies beyond the terminator of consciousness. Yet certain of the conscious elements of his experience smack of the religious. Is this kind of faith-experience truly from God? In this case the pastor can undoubtedly provide help for the client in interpreting his experience, for theology offers a number of useful criteria for guidance.

A prolific writer on spiritual and mystical theology, Jean Gerson (1363-1429), chancellor of the University of Paris, offered three basic and simple signs for judgment: doctrine, associates, objectives.

Can what the subject consciously experienced be integrated with orthodox doctrine and sound theology? Is his experience an objectification not merely of what he himself believes, but of what is rightly accepted by the Christian community?

Secondly, how has his experience affected his relationship with others? Is he able as a result of it better to incarnate elements of the gospel message? How do his companions react to him and his actions? Have they noticed any change in him that might have resulted from his experience? Is this for the better or worse?

Thirdly, what does the subject see the meaning of his experience to be? Has it given him new purposes or objectives in life? Has he been able to attain any of these? Has this attainment brought him a greater personal fulfillment and his associates greater satisfaction with him?

In addition to these medieval criteria, which are largely indirect and general, the theology of more recent times has presented several others which are more directly coupled to the experience itself, and linked more closely with the likely components of it.

Obviously faith must enter into the formula for judging religious experiences in a way other than that in which Gerson used it. How has the experience affected the faith of the subject? Has faith been deepened, rendered more lively and efficacious? If so, here is a positive sign. If, on the other hand, the experience has produced a faith-obsession with itself, belief in it as God-given is contraindicated. Genuine religious experience also promotes greater confidence in and reliance upon God. All the manuals of spiritual theology so contend, but we might add that this should also result in an increase in self-respect and self-confidence. Many of the biblical heroes who had experiences of theophanies manifested a remarkable self-reliance. Abraham dared to bargain with God; Moses demanded a sign; Jeremiah made bold to upbraid the Lord, etc. The over-all strengthening of faith and trust in God and in himself should advance the subject's apprehension of the meaning of life in terms of gospel values. His courage and stamina in the face of difficulties and death itself will be enhanced, and he will not easily be shaken by criticism or rejection, save perhaps where he has a right to expect help and support—from his minister. The effect of the experience upon the charity of the subject offers in the ultimate analysis the best criterion. The pastor might seek to ascertain not only if his client feels a deeper and more involving love for God such as might incline him to pray more frequently and more fervently, but also how his love of self and neighbor have fared as a result of the experience. To love one's neighbor as oneself implies that one have a deep respect and concern for oneself as well as an ability to empathize with one's fellow-man, to conduct oneself, as Martin Luther once said, as if one's neighbor's weaknesses, faults, sins and foolishness were one's own.

The humility of the client remains an additional important factor to be considered. Spiritual writers have stressed this virtue as an almost inevitable result of divine visitation. One should be able to see oneself in a more objective light. Without exaggeration or conceit one senses a heightening of the perception of one's own true worth. Withal, limitations and faults are acknowledged without defensiveness or excuse; this too is a characteristic operational mode of the virtue of humility.

Writers like St. Benedict attribute to humility the power to drive out fear and insecurity. Some theologians consider it to be a kind of counterpart to or double of charity. St. Francis de Sales terms charity humility that ascends on high, and humility charity that comes down from above. The great expert on the mystical life, St. John of the Cross, points out that the more a person humbles himself in both body and soul, the more completely he can be united to God.

Deep joy and contentment too spring from an experience of the divine. Happiness can suffuse the depths of the psyche, notwithstanding doubts, anxiety and even suffering at more peripheral levels of consciousness. The Father of German mysticism, Meister Eckhart, sees God as essentially a being who laughs and plays, who exults and rejoices in his creation, and imparts peace and happiness to those whom he visits. Every creature, he says, is an admixture of bitterness and honey-sweetness. The bitterness can be skimmed off the surface, and then the honey-sweetness that comes from God will be discovered. St. Francis de Sales, too, traces God as the source of joy and contentment. He points out that a person who eats a bonbon cannot say that his mouth is sweet, but only that the candy is sweet. So human joy and contentment put one on the track of God.

A truly spiritual experience, as the experts testify, brings to the psyche a certain flexibility and resiliency. One of the notes of both a drug-induced and neurotic peak experience is the rigidity that it produces in the subject. He is "hooked." And this fact promotes unusual behavior and, ultimately, notable changes in personality. The modality of his response to life situations is perceptibly narrowed. On the contrary, the personality of the subject who has had an authentic religious experience is enriched and fulfilled.

The genuine religious experience, though engendering a desire for recurrence, does not create a dependency in the subject. Rather it enhances his ability to act from native feeling. It encourages self-activation, and reduces the need for heteronomous guidance. It fosters genuine spontaneity. It facilitates a fuller expression of feeling, makes the subject less inhibited, less self-centered, less introverted. The pastor will consider it a good sign if his client is able eventually to resolve his own doubts, if all he seeks from his counsellor is the necessary information to make his own decision, not the judgment or encouragement of the man he considers an expert.

A real experience of God provides great incentive for meaningful and useful action. It vectors one toward the creation of some useful project or the actualization of some beneficial plan. It abets the realization of good desires. It gives one a sense of greater freedom even though he is enthralled both by the experience itself and what it leads to or impels him to do. It is a truly liberating experience.

Divine grace provides for a possibility of greater intimacy both with God and one's fellow-man. It inhibits the focussing of attention on the risks involved in such an enterprise, and opens up or expands the mind to see new opportunities for more frequent and more fruitful contacts. It allays fears of futility or embarrassment. Grace gives new meaning to pre-existing bonds of service and friendship. It stimulates an experience that is uplifting and bolstering.

Finally, the experience of God is fundamentally pleasurable. The gratification it brings will impel the subject to seek its recurrence. It will whet his appetite for even greater, more transcendent and more enduring experiences of the same kind in the future. Though feelings of apprehension, fear and anxiety may at first be aroused, eventually they will be swallowed up in the over-all pleasurable feelings that will ensue.

By the application of these criteria even a doubtful experience of God may at length be apprehended as authentic and real. It will then bear the same note of authority and imperativeness that the easily recognizable experience entails. If not from the data that protrude from the dark area of consciousness, then at least from the clear and fully distinguishable characteristics presented in the focus of awareness, it will be perceived as a mediated experience. And its source will be recognized as God.

The genuine religious experience is one which gives a person an opportunity for transcendence while at the same time rooting him more fully in both himself and God. Through it one is helped to establish his own personal identity as well as his oneness with Christ. In the celebration of the Christian mysteries, by symbolically dying and rising with Christ, by eating his flesh, by "putting him on" in the words of St. Paul, the believer professes not merely his union, but identity with Christ; he becomes a Christian, a Christ. The true religious experience reflects this fact, and so can become in the life of the believer a framework for his spiritual orientation and devotion.

The second question raised by peak religious experience relates to the reality of God. As we said, this is more a theological than pastoral issue. If in a religious experience I can apprehend God as a real being, then the traditional proofs for the existence of God become superfluous for me. As we said, what is grasped as real in experience, certainly exists for the one who has the experience. His experience is in no sense a proof, to be sure. Proofs are logical structures, and experience is preconceptual. But experience is much more satisfying than proof. Proofs are necessary only for what cannot be experienced. If what is encountered in an experience of God is his reality and not just some projection of self or some structure of awareness itself, then the question of proofs for the existence of God will become an irrelevant one for theology.

The believer can simply proclaim that God exists because through an experience of grace his presence was felt. Proofs might still be considered necessary for those who never have such an experience, but if every man is given a chance for salvation, and for salvation some kind of belief in God is required, we must presume that this grace is given to every man. We must conclude that every person is provided with at least the remote opportunity to have such an experience at some time in his life.

Orthodox theology has always taught that the real God is totally other, that he is in no way fully comprehensible to man on earth. He is not precisely and completely definable in terms of conscious data. St. Paul says that we see him now as through a glass darkly. If the real God is present in the experience of man it must be in that dark area, in that vast expanse that lies beyond the terminator of consciousness. For our conscious life revelation and theology have created for us a handy surrogate of God, an abstract and metaphysical God who results from the traditional *via negationis* (e.g., not limited like his creatures, and so infinite; not changeable like his creatures, and so immutable, etc.) or an anthropomorphic God who arises from the application of the *via analogiae* (loving like man, but not exactly in the same way; knowing like man, but not in exactly the same way, etc.). The biblical trend in theology today moves us away from the more metaphysical *via negationis* and toward the more scriptural *via analogiae*. For the God of revelation is pictured in human form. He has a voice; he becomes angry; he loves and hates; he grows sad; he persuades and argues. The first few pages of the Bible tell the Hebrews that man is created in the image and likeness of God. Man himself is the best analogy of God that creation supplies. The ancient pagans wanted to have concrete pictures or statues to show worshipers what their gods looked like. So they made idols. The promoters of religion in ancient times were not naive enough to believe that these idols were actually the gods themselves; they were understood to be only the images of the gods. But because in their very form they captured some of the mystery and numinosity of the invisible god himself, they also were adored and worshiped. If the ancient Egyptians, for example, wanted to know how to picture in their minds the gods Horus, Anubis and Thoth, the idols showed them. They all had human bodies, but Horus had the head of a hawk, Anubis the head of a jackal, and Thoth the head of an ibis. According to G. von Rad, the Hebrew word which is translated as "image" in Genesis 1:26 ("Let us make man into an image and likeness of ourselves") can also mean idol. The Hebrews were forbidden to make idols, and the reason for this is clear. Man is the only idol of God that there can be. Only man himself can in some way capture the special numinosity of the divinity. The ancient Hebrew like his pagan counterpart wanted also to see what his God looked like. The primitive revelation of God tells him in effect: "If you want to know what I look like, look at your neighbor: then you will know; and if you want to honor me, honor also your fellow man."

This ancient revelation was, of course, fulfilled, perfectly verified and made even more normative in the Christian doctrine of the Incarnation. Here a man was not only the idol or image of God. Here man is indeed God. From its very beginning in Hebrew thought to its culmination in Christianity revelation set about to convert the original *homo homini lupus* into *homo homini deus*. The surrogate of God useful to consciousness is patterned after man.

This surrogate of God, then, does not represent the idolatrous whim of any individual or limited group. It is sanctioned by revelation. It is hallowed by the fact that it has provided meaning for life itself in endless generations of large segments of the human race. Indeed, if we consider the fact that even those primitive pagan peoples who use animals, who use figures other than human ones for images of their gods, endow these non-human idols with human qualities, cathect them with brotan potential, we can see this useful surrogate of God as an archetype that is the product of the collective unconscious of mankind itself.

But man is perceived to be a mysterious admixture of blatantly obvious characteristics that easily appear in consciousness, and a surprisingly far-reaching hidden potential for transcendence that, precisely as potential, lies beyond the terminator of consciousness. What appears in consciousness may well ground the perception of this useful surrogate of God. What is contained in the abyss of transcendence beyond the terminator may well respond to the total otherness of the real God. Along the terminator of consciousness this mystic abyss of transcendence, the God who is totally other, can become partially coterminous with the conscious and definable characteristics of the useful surrogate of God.

Like the real God (and unlike the abstract concept of being as such) this abyss is really not conceivable. But this does not mean that it cannot be an object of experience. Let us use the analogy of space to illustrate this point. Like the unlimited reaches of space itself, when this abyss is conceived by the mind, it has to be represented as something positive and limited. Thus it becomes a mental construct, an abstraction, a representation that is incomplete and relational, exhibiting only one or other aspect of the total and absolute reality it stands for. Indeed, the fact that it can be represented only by a construct or surrogate automatically inserts a doubt in the reflective mind as to whether it is real or not. We can ask whether unlimited space is a reality or not. But the initial, unreflective reaction of the mind, and the primitive reaction of the unsophisticated mind, is to consider it as real. There is nothing apparently more real than space. In it I live, and act and have my being; and it does seem to be unlimited, infinitely divisible down into the microcosm and indefinitely expansible into the macrocosm. But upon further reflection we note that, in the way we conceive of it, its reality is ambiguous. In reflection it may or may not be perceived as real. The modality of our representation, paradoxically enough, cannot correspond to the reality if it is real; and yet it is only through that modality of representation that space can be conceived of as real. The doubt about the reality is introduced by the paradoxical nature of the mechanism of knowing which must relate what is conceived to what appears in the bright area of consciousness, and hence perceive it as limited by the terminator. The mind in considering the possibility that unlimited space can be real must render a judgment, which emanates from concepts or reflections that are in turn based upon experience. But the experience of space itself, of course, has to be pre-conceptual. And it can be analyzed as one of both positive and negative space. But when space is conceived, only positive space, that is, the space that appeared in my experience as lying on this side of the terminator of consciousness, is represented. Conscious space has to be limited and positive. The unconscious element of the experience, that is, the experience of a void, or negative space, space lying beyond the terminator of consciousness (which, if conceived, must be thought of as positive, and so limited in some way) can also be reflected upon. In a spontaneous reflection that unconscious void or negative space appears as both unlimited and real. The terminator of consciousness perceived as a limit is the key factor in this experience. It sets up the "non" with relation to what lies beyond it.

The simultaneous perception of the limitedness of consciousness and the possibility of consciously (and thus really) transcending that limit to find something experientially real grounds and validates any subsequent reflective conception of both the absolutely unlimited and totally other (in the case of space, its negativity) reality. It is the presumed reality of the "non" in experience, defined and created by the terminator of consciousness that is the foundation for what is perceived to be a valid idea of the unlimited and totally other, that is, that which is neither identical nor analogous. Because what lies beyond the terminator of consciousness can actually be experienced, it is spontaneously conceived of as real, and not just a mental construct or projection to be played with in abstract mathematical games. Indeed if this transliminally grounded insight is in no sense related to reality, then no valid epistemology can be constructed, science is an illusion, and discovery by serendipity becomes chimerical. The dimensionality of consciousness itself (which will be considered in greater detail in the last chapter) assures the reality of both as yet undiscovered space and future time.

We must insist that what lies beyond the terminator of consciousness is not merely the foundation for a valid concept of being as such, although it is certainly connected with the concept of being. What is perceived is not only unlimited in the order of being, but precisely neither univocal with nor even analogous to conceived being; in other words, it gives the impression of being totally other. Perhaps the phrase of Paul Tillich and some other modern theologians "the ground of being" would be the one best to characterize it. While the concept of being is recognized as emanating from the operation of the mind, the experience of the totally other, if and when it is had, is seen in reflection as having been produced from outside of the psyche.

This issue of the terminator of consciousness raises the question of the nature of consciousness itself. The idea that consciousness *per se is* unlimited (and of course, totally other to physical reality) was advocated in ancient times, and is related to certain beliefs like those of the Buddhists today. Heraclitus, Empedocles, Plato and the Neoplatonists, medieval thinkers like F. Patrizi, M. Ficino, G. Cardano, G. Bruno and others advanced the idea of a world-soul in such a way as to imply the existence of some kind of cosmic consciousness. This notion of panpsychism is not at all unknown in the writings of certain of the eastern Fathers of the Church who were influenced by Neoplatonism. Even St. Augustine mentions it, though he treats it with a kind of tentativeness.

Pierre Teilhard de Chardin in explaining his concept of the "within" of things reflects upon the tendency of matter to spiral in on itself, and views it as an incipient kind of consciousness in the stuff of the universe itself. For him the centeredness of conscious life and the synthetic, complexifying vectoring of the matter are but two connected segments of one and the same reality.

Apart from theory, though, whether old or new, man does experience his consciousness as *de facto* limited. To be sure, consciousness itself evidences a highly complex and multifarious concatenation of limiting factors as we pointed out in the chapter on experience. Very often one of the first experiences a person will have will be of himself as limited, and this will lead to the definition of himself as person. Yet though experience testifies that consciousness is ultimately quenched at every level of its concrete extension, it also witnesses a continual transcendence of these limits, as we have indicated, not only for the individual, but for society at large. It may well be that this possibility of transcendence not only grounds theories of panpsychism that history recounts, and a sense of the participatory nature of individual consciousness that oriental mysticism and, to some extent, Teilhardianism presuppose, but also introduces a person to the concept of his own limitation and dependency as a springboard reaching ultimately to the notion of God as the infinite and absolute being.

We have indicated that one of the commonly perceived phenomena in any peak experience is a kind of awareness of a union of opposites. Such awareness often occurs in peak experience that has religious overtones; or, perhaps it is this very factor that gives a religious flavor to certain peak experiences. Cardinal Nicholas of Cusa linked the phenomenon of union of opposites with the divine. He wrote that only in infinity can there be an opposition of things opposed without opposition. Only in God can opposites, remaining what they are, be united. Thus he stated that in God to have is to be, to move is to stand, and to run is to rest. It might be quite natural for a person, aware in his experience of his own limits, and at the same time sensing the transcendence of consciousness that the concrete perception of a union of opposites implies, to feel that he has been in contact with the infinite.

A whole constellation of data linking a person's awareness of limitation to the divine might indeed be amassed, but the brightest star will always be the one that shines from the darkness beyond the terminator of consciousness. For here and here only can contact be made with not just the useful surrogate of God when man desires it, but with the real God when he desires it.

At this point we can introduce the fourth central thesis of this essay. The real God appears not in the filled spaces, but in the holes in human reality. This is the reason why he seems to some to be a mere projection of man's needs, desires and wishes. But the fact that appears to be warranted by experience is that God actually does seem more real to people in time of trouble or distress, when attention is sharply focussed upon human limitation. At this time especially the useful surrogate of God seems almost to be transformed into the real God. The God of religion becomes the God of life and personal meaning. The concept of God may well at this time be enfleshed in experience.

Here again we must assert that by this theological analysis we are not constructing any proof for the existence of God. What we have said is obviously no proof for the existence of God any more than it is a proof for the existence of unlimited space. Nor are we espousing ontologism. We are not at all advocating the theory that there is some kind of innate idea of God. We are operating at the level of awareness and non-awareness, at a level of experience that is prior to all ideas or conceptualizations, and consequently prior to all judgments about existence or non-existence. We are merely analyzing common basic reflections upon the reality of what is experienced at times as lying beyond the terminator of consciousness.

And we are saying that the first native or spontaneous reaction in such a reflection is to consider not only such a peak experience itself, but also what is perceived in it on both sides of the terminator of consciousness to be real. So we are proposing for consideration the idea that in experience at times some contact can be had with what can be spontaneously identified as the real God, whereas in logical, conceptual life it is possible for one to contact only the useful surrogate of God which represents the real God only by way of negating abstraction or analogy.

If such contact with the real God is actually had by a person in his experience, then, of course, the actual existence of the real God is very likely no longer to be an issue for that person. He will not deny the existence of what he experiences and can at least in some way identify in his experience.

But our analysis has been directed at the theologian who would want an explanation of how the real God could contact such a person. The theology of the past has almost exclusively considered such a contact to be possible only through concepts, or the action of God upon mind and will. It failed largely to coordinate its theories with the data of psychology. It had to consider the God of metaphysics, a useful surrogate of God, as the real God simply because it was not sufficiently outfitted with psychological apparatus to cope with experience. It could not admit the possibility of an unconscious or not fully conscious experience. And so it had ultimately to flee to concepts and logic.

Through our analysis of the operation of the terminator of consciousness in experience we hope we have presented for further consideration and study the germ of a new existential and experiential theological theory.

5

DAILY RELIGIOUS EXPERIENCE

Many are convinced that our age is witnessing a decline in religiosity. People do not seem to have that "old time religion." No longer is the Church as much a part of their lives as it was in the past. Attendance at services is waning. Young people are turned off by the kind of ethic the Church inculcates, as well as by its seeming phoniness evidenced by the discrepancy between its preaching and its practice. People do not seem to be praying the way they used to. The "new theology" has confused many formerly devout Christians; they have been told that their practices are no longer relevant. The flight of priests and ministers to other occupations has scandalized some of their parishoners. Demythologization of the gospel and the secularizing trend in the Church have robbed great numbers of people, if not of their faith, at least of those religious expressions to which they were accustomed in the past. The controversy over the birth control issue in the Roman Catholic Church has resulted in a loss of prestige for the magisterial authority. Failure to do something about the leadership vacuum in the hierarchy has resulted in abdication of considerable power to pressure groups in the Church.

The professional sociologists and pollsters admit that it is difficult to measure a thing like religiosity. What is more difficult is to compare present religious fervor with past; very few and very limited polls of this nature were taken in times past. Some do assert, however, that the impressions many people have about a current decline are without basis in fact. The statistical data which are available indicate a continuity in the quality of American religious feeling and practice. The Church of the present is not radically different from its predecessor of decades ago. There have always been secularizing tendencies, challenges to authority, new devotions, and shifts of theological emphasis. If anything, the turmoil in the Church today has produced a more meaningful dialogue between clergy and laity which has resulted in a more professional approach to ministry and a consequent greater involvement of the layman in religious activity.

Radical theological movements like the notion of the death of God are now on the wane. Perhaps this is due to the fact that people have never apprehended it precisely as a theology. One of its prophets, Gabriel Vahanian, rightly intimates that it does not really tell us anything about God at all. True to modern anthropotropism in theology, it is aimed at man. So some sociologists of religion consider it a kind of psychological projection betokening a sort of death of man in society. It is the symbolized symptom of American social anomie, the rapidly accelerating disruption of the traditional American way of life. It remains a *de facto* indicator of the demise of the old societal norms and structures, though it actually purports to stimulate social ideals in making man feel his responsibility for the world, in apprising him of the fact that he has come of age, in telling him that he is master of his own destiny and the shaper of the universe in which future generations will have to live. Theothanatism is a kind of psychedelic *Zeitgeist* projected by radical and revolutionary American society today to facilitate the repression of guilt feelings resulting from its failure to preserve the sacred heritage and patrimony of the past. It tells us that God is really man's failure. Christian religiosity has been a surrogate for faith. Its sweetness has dulled man's taste for the red meat of authentic witness, for that witness which bespeaks true adherence to the gospel message. Man must take seriously the injunction of Genesis: he must become master of the universe. The strings of creation have been cut. The world is man's, and man must be ready to assume responsibility for it. The image of God in his heaven and man on his earth must be reversed. If in the past man has anthropomorphized God, that was possible, as Gollwitzer says, only because God had first theomorphized man. But men would really rather believe in anything than in their own humanity.

Today more than ever men do, however, seek self-definition by action. Many are suspicious of the past. They admire its absolutist ideologies, and perhaps secretly wish for similar ones for our times. But they fear disillusionment. The glory of the past has been debunked, demythologized. And there seems to be no possibility of attaining certainty or even consensus in the present. To commit oneself today would perhaps be ultimately to cop out. To hang loose and hope for a breakthrough is the only tolerable stance. But until the breakthrough occurs, each one must be free to do his thing and find himself, his true identity, in doing it.

In such an atmosphere it might even seem totally irrelevant to speak about daily religious experience. If radical theology, the theology of action, is passing away, and if there is no desire to return to the practices of the past, what is left, except perhaps to follow the advice of Camus, and believe in nothing to make it possible for anything to happen? The fact that statistics show no appreciable decline in religiousness today despite what is happening in society might, however, indicate something significant. The quest for religious sentience seems to be on the upswing. Interest in the occult, in astrology, in oriental mysticism, in all types of bizarre religious experience is mounting. Today's world is not very high on theory or philosophy, particularly if it emanates from the past, but it does have regard for experience of all kinds in its search for self-definition by action.

If people today are having peak experiences of a religious nature, one might well suspect that they are also having ordinary, day-to-day religious experiences as well. As we said, one of the characteristics of a peak experience is that it effects some kind of significant change in routine behavior. The perception of an altered behavior pattern in virtue of a mind-blowing kind of encounter with God might well make one aware of the fact that his daily life has been impregnated with religious significance. But as the German philosopher Friedrich Nietzsche pointed out, the highest values tend ultimately to devaluate themselves. As new behavior patterns become well established, the connection of them with former experience, even peak experience, tends to grow more obscure, and maybe eventually to be lost entirely. Unless the peak experience can be integrated with other religious operatives in the life of a person, its magic charm will gradually be dissipated until it ultimately becomes just an interesting topic of conversation for idle moments or chance meetings with ministers at cocktail parties.

The only guarantee for a regularly continuing religious experience is the abiding presence of specifically religious factors in the daily life of believers. I have discussed at great length the whole question of divine presence and psychological elements associated with it in my former book entitled *A Contemporary Theology of Grace*. It will suffice here just to sketch a few ideas from this work. Presence is really a function of awareness. Things do not just become present. They are made present by the consciousness. Or rather, the consciousness makes itself present to them. I direct my awareness to myself and things outside of myself and so render them present to me. And normally it is with reference to some particular facet of my self-awareness that I create presences. Sometimes these facets are fully conscious, as for instance, if I am a racing buff and think of horses all day. Often they are unconscious, as in the case where I always think of my father when I meet a certain teacher. An important element in an experience of presence is the empathy, or feeling of contact with the person or object which is rendered present. Some psychologists believe that this contact is established by the operation of an archetype, or collator of feeling. It does for sentience what the universal concept does for thinking. It unifies experience so that the subject will, as it were, know how to feel in different circumstances. The archetype is characterized by an aura of completeness, numinosity, complexity and ambivalence, absoluteness and permanency. As such it is more of a cultural or social than an individual phenomenon. Jung sees it as emanating from the collective unconscious. In the past, various archetypes have been used to assure a continuous awareness or presence of religious teachings. Jesus spoke of the kingdom (king archetype). Unlike other nations, the Jewish people of his time had no king or kingdom. God had promised them a great leader; yet they were under the domination of foreigners; they were totally subservient to Rome. How galling this was to the proud people who considered themselves Yahweh's own! Is this how he took care of them? Every time they heard of the injustice or cruelty of some Roman official, every time they saw a soldier or emblem of Rome, they felt the desire for a kingdom of their own, a kingdom like that of a Solomon or David in times past. But at that very time they would become aware of the promise of Jesus too. No wonder they were so sorely disappointed when Jesus announced openly that his kingdom was not to be of this world!

Through his parables Jesus cathected familiar objects with a sentient relationship to the archetype. These became symbols evoking the archetype's numinous activity in the lives of the people. The fisherman could not cast his nets nor the farmer sow his seed nor the shepherd feed his flock without thinking of Rome and the kingdom promised by Jesus. Jesus made use of the secular to render present the religious. He was indeed a master teacher. His methodology was fully orientated toward the experiential.

But is there any possibility of imitating Jesus today? Are there any clearly identifiable archetypes that can be used for religious purposes in our society? The archetype is indeed a dangerous tool; it can backfire. It is essentially ambivalent. But withal, it might be worth the risk if a new era of religiousness is to dawn. What are the issues that turn people on today? Do they unify or polarize people? Can they be used for religious purposes?

Even in our complex society we observe a tendency for homogeneous groups of people to settle together. The pastor who really gets to know them, to understand their goals and needs, their interests and feelings, and to empathize with them as well, might well be able to discover some archetype that will be as effective for him in creating religious experience as the archetype of the kingdom was for Jesus. He may uncover symbols in the daily lives of his people that will constantly keep before them certain elements of the gospel message. He may do much to create in his people an abiding presence of God.

If the archetypes and symbols that were considered to have had some religious value, those associated with human origins and destiny, are not as active in our society today as once they were, the ones associated with the establishment of identity, both personal and societal, are assuming a greater importance. The search for identity and the establishment of healthy interpersonal relationships are key factors in the dynamics of everyday life today. Origins refer to the unverifiable past; destiny looks to the uncertain future; identity has to do with the real now. Perhaps for this very reason statistics do not show a staggering decline in church attendance today. For ritual provides a religious experience which allows a worshiper to assume a new identity and through it clarify his own. Ceremonial leaves both the past and the future happily undefined, though it undoubtedly is related to both. It is a re-enactment of the past, but of that past which is so mystic, sacral and numinous as to defy academic debunking and escape historical criticism. It is a taking hold of the future, but that future which the believer sees as secure, unshakable, ecstatic and inevitable, a future that lies beyond the boundaries of this world. But it is most especially a *now*, a religious experience that prompts the worshiper to consider who he is in the eyes of God and his Church.

The sacraments of initiation and the Eucharist highlight in their ritualistic symbolism the mystical identification of the worshiper with Christ. They imply that by indulging in this ritual identification with Jesus the believer is better able to establish his own identity, to understand just who he is, what is his dignity, and what is his job in the world today.

In baptism the candidate symbolically becomes Christ by doing the thing of Christ. He celebrates and appropriates as his own Christ's paschal mystery. Ritualistically he dies and rises with Christ. He dies to his former sinful self, to his old ways of acting. He rises to a new life, the life of Christ himself in which he now shares. He believes he has Christ's own task to complete in the world. He is one with Christ and those who have similarly identified themselves with Christ in his paschal mystery. Has he therefore had a moving religious experience? Unfortunately for most, no, because the odds are that they were baptized as infants when they could not possibly appreciate what was happening. The only possibility for them is to discover later what happened to them in the greatest moment of their lives.

When infant baptism became the rule, fortunately the sacrament we call confirmation was separated from it. Through its distinctive symbolism this initiatory sacrament would convey the same message that was given at baptism, only now at a time when it could be understood by the recipient. So it could be an occasion of a meaningful religious experience, albeit one that occurs only once in a lifetime.

Unhappily, however, today in the minds of many there is some confusion about the real significance of the symbolism of this sacrament. The unclarity arises largely from the name given it in the western Church in recent times. We call it confirmation. In the eastern Church it is Anointing or Chrism. The early western Church used the terms Sign or the Signing.

Among the ancients olive oil was used for lighting and to a certain extent for heating purposes. It was considered to be a source of great energy. The athlete applied it to his muscles before a contest. Not understanding the nature of the epidermis and layers of skin and tissue under it, the ancients had the idea that this oil, penetrating down into the musculature, would bestow the extra energy needed for extended exertion. Symbolically the athlete's oil was employed in the early church to anoint the bodies of those going down into the waters of baptism. There one was to encounter not just an opponent in the sporting arena, but the enemy of all mankind himself. For this struggle extra strength was needed. The believer's resolution to go through with this struggle needed to be confirmed. So olive oil, the oil of catechumens, was used to symbolize the superhuman strength required to do this task, to do the thing of Christ, to accept death and so one's humanity, and to rise to a new life with Christ. This balm signified the strength that God bestowed upon the candidate to accomplish well the paschal mystery.

The ancients also used a sweet, aromatic oil called *myron* in Greek. It served well as a deodorant or perfume. *Myron* was often used by prominent or public officials when they were initiated into the ministries they were to perform for the people. This was the kind of balm poured over the hair of kings and priests. The idea was, of course, that those who had some kind of public charge ought not to be offensive in any way to the people they served. Their lives ought to have a sweet smell about them, not the stench of corruption and venality. This oil was given the name chrism by the Christians when it was used ritualistically by them.

Jesus was the messiah. He was the one anointed with this sweet-smelling oil to perform a service for his people. *Christos* is the Greek word signifying an anointed one, the translation of the Hebrew word messiah. Christians are so called because the Jesus-oil, chrism, is poured over their heads. In baptism they identified themselves with Christ. Again in the Signing this identification is proclaimed. Chrism is poured over their heads to signify that they are messiahs, anointed ones, christs. Their lives ought to be redolent with the sweet odor of Christ.

They have his very own job to continue and complete. They have taken upon themselves the very same ministry that he had. The world will behold no other Christ but the one it sees in them. The sacrament of Signing, confirmation, can provide a religious experience for the man of our times. It is eminently concerned with the now, though linked mystically with the numinous past, and portentiously with the apocalyptic future. It is a sacrament of self-identification; the recipient discovers his own identity in Christ. It is a sacrament of action: the recipient has Christ's own job to do in the world.

The Eucharist too is a sacrament relating to identity and action. And it can provide a daily religious experience to those who take advantage of it. The early Church realized that a person could be baptized only once. Re-baptism would destroy the symbolism of the sacrament. As a person can die and rise from death only one time, so this sacrament can be used only once. But what it implies is a truth so stupendous, so psychedelic that it ought to be repeated continously throughout life to be fully grasped. The believer is identified with Jesus himself! And he has the job of Jesus to accomplish in his own time and locale! What he symbolizes in the sacrament has to be accomplished by him in his life. God is counting on him to do his part in the project that was initiated for man in Jesus. And if he does not do it, it simply will not be done. It is not sufficient for him just to believe in Jesus; he has also to believe in himself and in God's power in him because the fact is that God believes in him and trusts him.

The Eucharist, like confirmation, is another mirror held up to baptism. It reflects to the believer none other than himself in transcendence, himself as he is identified with Jesus. It is primordial feedback; it is nourishment of what happened in baptism. The gifts that are offered in the Eucharist, bread and wine, symbolize the very lives of the participants. Those lives are sustained by food and drink. Over these gifts are pronounced the words: "This is my body; this is my blood." The participants are shown who they really are, what life they really live in virtue of their baptism. What happens in the liturgical drama with the gifts has happened in their real life through baptism. They are mystically identified with Jesus himself. Again when the participants receive Christ in communion this same truth is driven home. They introject Christ; they are in communion with him; they are one with him; they identity themselves with him as best they can through this ritual. And if they now know with whom they are identified, they know better who they are themselves and how they must act.

Apart from all ritualistic religious experience, there are indications that other kinds are also still significant to people in our time. It is the task of the minister to point these out also.

Many people embrace life with zest and do a great amount of good simply because they have discovered an ultimate meaning in their existence. They readily admit this of themselves if confronted, but often do not connect it with their religious life since they are not able to relate it to what we have called the useful surrogate of God. It is even more difficult for them to integrate it with that area of their experience to which it best corresponds, the perception of the real God along the terminator of consciousness. If a minister is skilled enough to take this rather common phenomenon and cathect it with religious significance through his sermons, counselling, parables and the example of his own life, he will have opened up to a considerable segment of his congregation a new area of religious experience.

A similar opportunity occurs in the case of people who are convinced about an over-all forward thrust to life. The genius of Pierre Teilhard de Chardin was that he could apply basic gospel notions to the progressive motion of biological evolution. He cathected a purely scientific theory with religious significance and thus not only enhanced its meaning for himself and others, but made this seemingly quite secular thing a source of religious experience.

There is still another significant area of human life which

contains a larval form of religious experience. Many people are able to relate the tragedies that occur in their lives to their own religious persuasions. Every minister knows that this is the time he is needed most, and can best do his thing. Man in trouble, if he has any faith at all, will turn to God. Even if he has no faith, this will be the time when he will be most vulnerable to a sales pitch for God. At this critical period of his life he will be more open than ever to sizing up what belief in God can offer him. It will be perhaps the only time that the idea of the victory of the cross will begin to make some sense to him. But people do not generally consider their own resiliency in such a situation as grounds for a religious reflection. They somehow just take in stride any optimistic rebound after tragedy. They do eventually get over the grief experienced at the loss of a father, mother or child. They are able to make do and adjust after suffering a serious financial loss. Yet, possibly because of an overemphasis in the past upon the theology of the cross, on self-denial and mortification, on humility and self-effacement, this rebound effect which certainly is perceived as some kind of transcendence, and might well be understood as a symbol of the resurrection, is not accounted as a religious experience.

In the experiences we have just considered, those of the ultimate meaningfulness of life, of the over-all forward thrust of life and of the optimistic rebound, the minister must be wary not to impose religious meaning by suggestion; it will not be valid unless it is discovered by the client in the experience itself. The theological expertise of the minister will guide him in helping the subject to evaluate such an experience. If a religious interpretation is forced, the needs of the minister undoubtedly will be met, but hardly those of the client, with the result that his future experiences of this kind will not be referred to God.

The very best and most common experience of God a person can have arises out of Christian love of neighbor. Such an experience corresponds perfectly with both the personalist and

activist trends of our times. It is related directly to the useful
surrogate of God in the awareness of the Christian which, as
we have indicated, is connected itself with the experience of
the real God that emanates from beyond the terminator of
consciousness.

As we said, man is the idol of God. The ancient revelation
tells us that we can have no other image of our God than man
himself. If we want to know what our God looks like, we have
only to direct our attention to ourselves and our neighbor.

This notion was greatly enhanced by the doctrine of the
Incarnation. God's Word, his own double image from within, identified himself with God's image from without; he became man. The identification of God with man became perfect
in the person of Jesus. Man is, as it were, the other of God, the
transcendence of God. It does not seem possible that the One
who is infinite, who is absolutely perfect in himself could
have any transcendence. Yet understood in the Pauline sense
of *kenosis*, emptying out of self, the self-transcendence of the
Word of God becomes plausible. And our faith tells us that
in Jesus it becomes fact.

God mortifies himself unto death in his kenotic Word. As
Rahner says, Jesus is *the* man, because of whom all other men
come to exist. Even in their limitations, in their sufferings, in
their sorrow and pain, in their tears and grief, in their death
itself, now, because of Jesus the *kenotic* divine Word, they
come to image God himself. Originally man reflected God
primarily in those facets of his existence that radiate his power
and glory: his ability to know all things, his freedom, his
mastery over the world. But in Christ, the fullest possible
revelation of God, man is seen to image God even better in
his littleness. It is, in the mind of Meister Eckhart, the humility
of a person that is the only vehicle he can use to move toward
the real God. The Father of German Mysticism is reputed to
have argued in this fashion: "The more I humiliate myself,
the more I exalt God. Humility is very much like a well; the
deeper it is, the higher and more exalted he appears who stands

on the top." The humbler a person is, the better he will be able to appreciate the real God. And the more he will be able to perceive in his own humanity and that of his neighbors the full revelation of the hidden God that Jesus is.

We have also indicated how the same basic message is given in liturgical cult. As we said, in ritual the believer identifies himself with Christ and so better establishes his own identity. If Christ is really the fullest revelation of God that man can expect in this world, and if the solidarity between Christ and other men is the main point of liturgical communication, then it should be easy to see how in encountering one's neighbor, one is also in some way encountering Christ. All human intercourse could in the light of this understanding become religious experience. In another person the Christian comes face to face with the image of Christ, with one who in a very real but mystic sense is the surrogate of Christ in the world, with one whom Christ has in a mysterious way identified with himself and so with the real God. "*I* was hungry, and you gave *me* food; thirsty, and you gave *me* something to drink; *I* was a stranger, and you took *me* home; naked, and you clothed *me*; sick, and you nursed *me*; a prisoner, and you visited *me* . . . when . . . ? Believe me when you did it to one of the least of my brothers here, you did it to me" (Mt 25, 35-40). Again: "Saul, Saul, why are you persecuting *me*?" (Acts 9: 4). Paul learned this lesson very well. It became one of the focal points of his evangelization. One might say that he pushed it to the utmost, to the verge of brashness and temerity when he wrote to the Corinthians: "Be imitators of me as I am of Christ" (I Cor 4: 16).

An early Christian writer, Marius Victorinus (who died sometime after 362), in his work entitled *Adversus Arium* advances the theory that Christ was the redeemer of all men precisely because, like Adam, he assumed a body and a soul that represented all mankind. This was Marius' way of expressing the idea that there was no human person in Christ. The humanity that the Word assumed was in a sense more representative of universal mankind than the humanity of any human person. God's dealings with man in Jesus were on the basis of humanity itself. No human person can ever stand in a one to one relationship to God. Jesus in his very being shows forth every man; he encompasses within himself all men, and so is able to be a new Adam who can act both in the name of and on behalf of universal mankind.

So too there emerged in the medieval morality plays the character Everyman, who is a kind of Christ-figure. For the great English mystic, painter and poet, William Blake, Jesus himself was really universal humanity. The creative genius in every man is the real savior of humanity; redemption is the mutual forgiveness extended from man to man.

St. Irenaeus in his *Adversus Haereses* views the appearance of the Word of God in human flesh as the verification and confirmation of the original revelation that man was indeed created in the image and likeness of God. But the visible Word, the incarnate Son of God, through his obedience to the Father also restored to mankind at large the capability of reflecting in the invisible, more significant facets of human life, in the life of grace, an even fuller and more astounding likeness of God. To know man as redeemed by Jesus is, in the best way possible to those who have not actually seen Jesus, to know God.

Scripture seems also to identify the love that one feels for one's fellow man as a truly religious experience, as an experience of God. "No one has ever seen God, but if we love one another, then God dwells in us!" (I Jn 4: 12). It is charity, love for one's fellow-man that is the foundation within the experience of the Christian for God's abiding presence. The liturgy has captured this idea in the chant for Holy Thursday: *"Ubi caritas et amor, Deus ibi est."* St. Augustine has developed many variations on the same theme. He says that the person who loves his neighbor has, by the very fact that he has experienced love, to love love itself. But as scripture testifies, God is love (I Jn 4: 6). So the love of God is necessarily bound up with the love of neighbor; one cannot love one's neighbor without at the same time expressing a love for God. He draws out this notion a bit further. By the very same charity that we love our neighbor, we love God. There are not two distinct loves; one of God and the other of neighbor, with some connection between them. What we might perceive as two distinct loves, are in fact identical, so that in loving one's neighbor one is in fact loving God. Indeed, St. Augustine goes so far as to intimate that a Christian does not really love his neighbor except through a power of love given to him by God himself. It is God's own love, his grace, that makes it possible for the Christian to love his neighbor in the way he does. "Love your neighbor, then," Augustine says, "and consider in yourself the origin of that love: there to the fullest extent possible, you will see God."

St. Francis de Sales has proposed a similar idea. He writes in his *Treatise on the Love of God* "To love our neighbor in charity is to love God in man." We do not just love our neighbor; in loving him we love God. And for the Christian this must be a conscious fact; it must become an object of experience that is brought out from the dark area beyond the terminator of consciousness. The motive of true charity demands some recognition of God in the act to the extent, at least, that one's neighbor is perceived as an image of God. In his *Letters* St. Francis writes: "It is not for the sake of the creature that you submit yourself to him, but for the love of God, whom you acknowledge in the creature."

Martin Luther argues that Christ really so identified himself with us and has so fully taken our part that it is as if he had actually been what we are. And in this he set an example for us. Every Christian has, in the words of Paul, to "put on Christ" by putting on his neighbor, that is, by so conducting himself toward him as if he were in the other's place. The mystic identity that is achieved in the Church between Christ, the Christian and his neighbor is precisely what is perceived by the believer as the most proper and fullest kind of religious experience.

The Jesuit theologians Vasquez and Ripalda some centuries ago and Rahner today advance the theory that there is no good act in the present economy of salvation that is not actually graced. By the very fact that I do what is good, I know that God's grace is with me. Every good and proper act can be, if I advert to it, an experience of God's grace at work in me, and consequently an experience of God present in my life.

The minister would like to help his people have a fuller and deeper experience of God in their daily lives. He knows that his role is precisely to point out to them the grace-situations in which they exist. He must seek out God's loving presence, his grace, even in the ordinary, the tawdry, the trivial. The effective minister is the one who learns how in faith and through study and personal development to convert triviality into ultimacy just as readily as he knows how in faith to convert a wafer of bread into the very substance of Jesus.

6

ROLE OF THE SPIRIT

Theology has always considered religious experience of whatever kind to be properly the work of the Holy Spirit in the human psyche. But today we find almost no area of the theological enterprise as uncultivated and underdeveloped as pneumatology. The undernourishment of Trinitarian theology itself down through the centuries is undoubtedly one of the reasons for this. The Platonistic matrix in which New Testament ideas about the multiplicity of persons in God initially waxed into a speculative theological system was only partially reformed in the thirteenth century through the widening influence of the Stagirite's philosophy upon theological thought. Because the Aristotelian system was fully orientated toward the intellectual, the eidetic elements in Trinitarian theology were stressed with the result that not much was said about the personal reality of the Holy Spirit. Movements like those of Joachim of Flora, the Beghards and Beguines, the Brethren of the Free Spirit and, later on, Meister Eckhart, though at times theologically aberrant, highlighted the orthodox position that the role of the Spirit was most important both in fostering the authentic memory of Jesus in tradition and in uniting and conforming the mystical body to its risen head. But largely the area of speculative pneumatology was left untouched even by these cultivators of the Spirit. In our own time the Pentecostal movement has taken up where these older views left off, but it too has failed to produce thus far any significant theological speculation about the function of the Holy Spirit, much less about his special personal reality.

The interest today in psychology with its tendencies to integrate rather than dichotomize knowledge and feelings and to see behavior as flowing from the whole person rather than from the distinct faculties of intellect, will and affectivity cries out for a further investigation of that divine person who is at one and the same time acknowledged as the most influential in the life of the Church of the post-Vatican II era and yet recognized as the most mysterious of all, indeed, the one whose very personality is not described in symbols readily associated with human experience, as are those of the Father and Son. The indulgence of the young people of our time in psychedelic drugs, in the psychomantic ascesis of oriental religions, and in deep, uninhibited personal encounters may well indicate a craving for some kind of pneumatic contact. But today's Christian minister may not find himself sufficiently versed in the lore of mysticism, or even well enough acquainted with the Spirit of Jesus to be able to be helpful, or to say anything significant.

Before we address ourselves to the question of the role of the Holy Spirit in religious experience, we must first consider briefly what current theology is saying about the function of the Spirit within the Trinity. The shift of emphasis in theology today from the purely intellectual to the experiential will make some difference as to even how we should conceive of the three persons, although it is not precisely our task here to lay down a whole new speculative basis for trinitarian doctrine. We can only touch lightly upon the issue.

The second person in the Trinity originates as a double or mirror-image of the first. But in an experiential setting the personhood, the conscious identity of each as distinct, is not to be considered apart from the third. For experience shows that identity can be established only in union. The Spirit of love which unites the two is also the Spirit which establishes their personal identity as well as his own in the very same act.

So in this framework it is easier to see than in a purely intellectualistic one why the Spirit is absolutely essential in a divine essence that is communicated to more than one person. The self-outside-of-self that the second person is would not be intelligible except in the light of the love that both unites and personally distinguishes the communicated self from the originating self. It is the Spirit that binds the I and I into a We, and by so doing sets over against each I a Thou. The Love that God is thus provides a common, or rather an identical, being-identity of the persons; but the way that love is vectored, the way it is expressed paves the way to the identification of the persons as really personally distinct. The goal or intentional source of this vectoring of love is the Spirit himself, who is thus himself established as a distinct person, but who in himself, in his personhood is the recipient in the order of execution, as it were, of the love originating in the other two persons. He originates as an actual and distinct person because, as we have seen, in loving each other (and thus establishing themselves as distinct persons in this union) the two persons must also love love itself and the goal of their love.

The role of the Spirit within the Trinity is one of imparting identity through the vectoring of his own personal numinosity, love. And it will be our contention that he plays the very same part in his functions *ad extra,* in religious experience.

Theologians have understood St. Paul's expression "the Spirit of Jesus" as signifying the chief role that the Holy Spirit exercises in the Church. He makes it come alive with the very life of Jesus. He sets norms for it so that it will not deviate from its evangelical mission, the mission that is Jesus'. He links it with the historical Jesus so that it will remain forever in authentic anamnesis of its founder. The Spirit has always been considered by theologians as the guarantor of stability in the Christian community as well as the living hermeneutic canon for the rendition of the gospel message itself amid the various vicissitudes of historical evolution. The immutability of the Spirit has been stressed in the reflections of the theology of yesteryear. The Spirit was likened to the human soul, which was seen as the source of constancy and continuity in life. The soul preserves the identity of the individual during the waxing and waning of his bodily form and function from birth to death. The day-to-day changes in appearance resulting from care and toil or joy and happiness do not really affect the identity of the individual, for that is assured by the presence of the self-same soul. So the Church, though quite protean in its historical development, remains always the Church of Jesus because it is informed by the Spirit of Jesus.

When we come to discuss the nature of spirit we are operating largely in the realm of abstractions. A spirit is for carnal man the most elusive of all being. The German philosopher Georg Hegel has defined it as that reality which preserves its identity precisely by being constantly other to itself. Material beings, on the other hand, maintain their identity by remaining always just exactly what they are. If indeed a spirit continuously escapes being just what it is, one may wonder if it is identifiable at all. Given the reality of its totally dynamic and fully relational nature, it still must be able to be comprehended, but only, of course, by the mind of another spirit. Its identity is pinpointed in the ratio of what it is to what it tends to be. Knowledge of the source of its *élan vital* and the location of its final goal provides the constants by means of which its vector can be plotted and contact established with it.

In a sense the ancients were better equipped linguistically than we are to deal with spiritual reality. In their most primitive sense the words employed by the peoples of classical times refer to the movement of the wind. Air is imperceptible until it begins to move. Then it is identifiable by its velocity and direction. So the essential dynamic and relational qualities of spirit are captured in the verbal analogy.

More particularly in some languages words denoting spirits were derived from the process of breathing. Air drawn into the body vivifies it and refreshes it. The expelled breath can set things in motion, can cool and resuscitate. The two Greek words largely employed in the New Testament to designate "spirit" are derived from forms which originally referred to the process of inhalation and exhalation.

We may not be aware of it, but the English words "psyche" and "suck" are linguistically related. Both can be traced to the Greek verb *psychō*. Later usage evidences an indiscriminate application of this verb to designate both inhalation and exhalation, but most likely it originally meant to draw in the breath, to suck in air. The Greek verb *pneō* and its corresponding noun-form *pneuma,* on the other hand, signify the blowing out of the breath. Thus the word *psychē* was seen by the ancients as particularly appropriate to express the spirit of man, which preserves its identity as spirit by becoming other to itself through drawing in external reality, through being constantly transformed in the assumption of new relationships to the outer world. But the word *pneuma* is used in the New Testament to designate the Holy Spirit. He is the spiration, the sigh of love, exchanged between the Father and the Son. While the *élan* of the human spirit is vectored inwards, the Holy Spirit's force moves in the opposite direction. He preserves his identity as a spirit by becoming other to himself in the external reality he transforms.

The New Testament may well indicate by its usage of these words that a kind of ideal coaptation between *psychē* and *pneuma* is possible when the human spirit breathes in and is vivified fully by the Spirit of God, who in turn fully suffuses and totally transforms such a receptive host. At least its language hints that the two spirits are directed toward each other, that they tend to achieve the otherness essential to their spiritual nature in each other. It stands to reason then that, if one is searching for the Spirit of God, the most likely place to find it is in the spirit of man. To be sure, man's spirit is fickle, and can identify with spirits other than God's. That is why spiritual writers have always been at pains to set up a system of norms for discerning spirits.

But, as St. Paul reveals, the Spirit of God, at least to the extent that we can experience him, is the Spirit of Jesus. He has his origin in the Logos and in the Father whose perfect image the Logos is. His goal in man is, as Paul also indicates, the recapitulation of all things in Christ, or in the words of Teilhard de Chardin, Christogenesis. His movement is always manward from God. He seeks to imprint the *eidos* (form) from which he takes his origin on the reality in which he becomes other to himself. So his vector is quite simply plotted. The Spirit of God is at work where the spirit of man is doing the "thing" of Jesus.

The German philosopher Friedrich Nietzsche hit upon a great Christian truth when he stated: "I wish men would begin to respect themselves; everything else would follow from that." But it was unfortunate that Christians themselves had for so long a time not recognized or fully acknowledged that truth. The Christianity they cultivated was loath to accept the weakness of the flesh. The onslaughts of Manichaeism, Catharism, and Jansenism left deep scars on the flanks of orthodoxy. The truly spiritual and holy person was seen as the one who could through detachment and mortification free himself as much as possible from the trammels of the flesh, and live as fully as terrestrial existence permitted in the realm of the spirit. The truly religious person could not accept without qualification or genuinely respect himself as he is, for his body was for him an occasion and source of caducity, sin, shame and guilt.

It is indeed amazing that the message of the gospel should have for so long a time been preached and heard and yet not fully understood. What is the pivotal truth of Christianity, the core doctrine that distinguishes it from every other religion? The Logos was made *flesh*. And it was that flesh that redeemed mankind. Can the death of Jesus on the cross, his law of brotherly love, his constant attempts to ease the intolerable burdens laid by the Pharisees on the shoulders of believers, his untiring inculcation and extollation of humility mean anything, if humanity as such, flesh as well as spirit, is not to be respected and accepted as sacred?

And did not the resurrection of Jesus point the way for true transcendence? Revelation shows that from the beginning man, because he is spirit as well as flesh, sought to escape from being just what he is. Adam wanted to be other to himself. He wanted to be like God. The Genesis legend captures most poignantly the dissatisfaction of man with himself that from the very beginning marks human history and sets man apart from all the rest of creation. Pagan religious literature is full of man's longing for immortality. Man wanted to escape death; he wanted to be divine. He desired to avoid that which precisely characterizes him as human and so inferior to the immortal gods. Pagan liturgy revolves around the idea of an oestrous cycle in nature whereby the divine tutelaries and patrons of worldly events reveal to man a constant resurgence of life, a possibility of survival after death. Man wanted this for himself. But Jesus demonstrated the only real way to transcendence. His doctrine his whole life, but most especially his death pointed out the truth that was indeed implicit in natural revelation, but to which man had blinded himself. Life comes only from death. Man can transcend himself only in accepting himself as he is. The real vehicle of his transcendence is his own humanity. If he seeks to apotheosize himself, he will fail; if he begins to accept himself as he is, he will most assuredly pass beyond himself. The simple and yet most astounding doctrine that Jesus preached was one that contradicted all the proud Greek philosophies, the fatuous pagan superstitions and the aberrant Jewish legalism of his time. He taught that it is his own mortal *flesh* that is the life of the world!

Karl Rahner has laid aside the theology that sees the Incarnation as a kind of divine afterthought effected to rectify the mess that man made of the world by sin. His view is more

Scotistic than Thomistic. He shows that as spirit God too seeks to be other to himself. The self-communication of God, his Logos, appearing as love in the void of nothingness outside of God, achieved that otherness when he was enfleshed. This enfleshed Logos was from the beginning the model, the pattern, after which all men were fashioned. So Rahner, like Nicholas of Cusa, Pico della Mirandola and other humanists before him, views man truly as the other of God. It is human flesh that is the link which permits God to attain otherness in creation and man to achieve transcendence in the sphere of the divine itself.

This paradoxical nature of the mystery that Christianity is has always been appreciated by men who in the past have searched out and contacted the Spirit of Jesus. As we saw, Meister Eckhart proposed the idea that only through humility can man really authenticate for himself the existence of God and actually render to him the divinity that is his due. And so, conversely, it is only with the truly humble that God can share his divinity. Man's thirst for apotheosis, for exalted otherness, can be quenched only in tasting and relishing himself as he really is.

Christianity then proclaims that the "thing" of Jesus is humanity itself. This is not to say that the doctrine of Christ is mere humanism, or that the Spirit of Jesus inspires any kind whatsoever of humanistic endeavor. Only that brand of humanism which confesses that Jesus is the Lord is authenticated by the Spirit. As Karl Barth wrote, if theology becomes totally humanistic, if God does not stand over against man as his creator and lord, the whole value of the Incarnation itself disappears, and the supreme dignity with which it endows mankind is lost. But, conversely, if religious values focus entirely on the divine and minimize the human, the work and significance of Jesus is made void. The gospels eluculently proclaim that the "thing" of Jesus is the humanizing of the proud structures that man has erected for himself in the pursuit of transcendence, and the facilitating of man's potential to accept and respect himself as he is.

As man becomes more human, God for him becomes more divine. As man devotes himself more and more to the doing of Christ's human "thing," God is better able to accomplish in him his divine "thing." The first principle for the discernment of spirits is set forth in the first letter of St. John (4:2): "This is the test by which God's Spirit is to be recognized: every spirit which acknowledges Jesus Christ as having come to us in human flesh has God for its author."

If the cultural currents of our day are sweeping men along toward a deeper and fuller appreciation of their humanity, then the time is ripe for the Church to heed the promptings of the Spirit and proclaim with ever increasing forcefulness that doctrine which is most central to and constitutive of Christianity at its core.

Ours is an era that cultivates personalism as well as humanism. People are groping for principles and techniques whereby they will be able to discover and develop their own personal identity. Our mental hospitals are filled to overflowing; psychiatrists' schedules are taxed to the limit; the market is glutted with psychological literature. Parents today are as preoccupied with the psychic health of their children as parents two or three generations ago were with the physical health of theirs. Permissiveness has become as much a part of the modern child's life as vaccination. The attention of our age is fixed upon the self. People want to know: "Just who am I? Why am I I and not someone else? How can I develop my personality?"

Modern psychological research reveals a number of characteristics that grace the mature or maturing personality. The first is relatedness. Personality cannot develop in isolation. Awareness of the self as self originates in the perception of other persons and the relationships one has with them. The closer, more frequent and richer the contact one has with others, the better will be the possibilities for a personal development that will result in a clear-cut, sharply defined, well-honed identity. The second is centrality. The mature person is rooted in himself. He belongs to himself first, and that is why he is not afraid to give himself to others. He feels good about himself. His own identity provides a framework of reference for the values he cherishes. He is able to devote himself to the pursuit and cultivation of these values. He respects both himself and what he stands for. The third is transcendence. Maturity implies the capacity to be open to new ideas, new values, new identities. The healthy person will constantly seek not only to be himself, but to be other to himself, to transcend what he is, to risk being what he is not. Within the limits of basic loyalty to his inner core-self, he will grow outwards and experience in this growth a reinforcement of his own identity.

The Christian message traditionally has highlighted solidarity with Jesus and so with the divine Logos not merely on the basis of a common humanity, but also, in a most astounding fashion, through the medium of a kind of personal identity with him. The Church is the mystical body of Jesus, and its individual members are appropriately termed, in the words of the great Alexandrian Father St. Cyril, "other Christs." This mysterious personal identity of Christians with Christ is, as we have pointed out, set forth dramatically in the liturgy. The life as well as the belief of Christians is epitomized in the proclamation of the paschal mystery at Mass: "Christ has died; Christ is risen; Christ will come again." The cross, the resurrection and ascension of Jesus tells the Christian both that he must be Jesus and how to be Jesus.

Man will begin to respect himself when he begins to experience more fully the presence of God's Spirit within him. That Spirit is reassuring him that he has an identity with Jesus. Not only is the divine Logos his brother in the flesh, but the very person of Jesus is in some mysterious way revealed to the world today in his own human flesh. In assuming this identity with Jesus, of course, man does not lose his own, nor deny the historical Jesus his. For basically the identity of the Christian with Jesus is an identity of union, a union that is not merely moral, as among members of the same family, nor grossly physical, as if the Church were a new superbody of Jesus, but totally unique, describable only as mystical or numinous, as unique and mysterious as the Incarnation itself. And modern psychological research has shown that the closer persons are united, the more they identify with each other, the better each is able to be centered in himself, to recognize and consolidate his own distinct personhood and grow in it.

The task of the minister today is to show the Christian people just who they are. It is to make men more aware of the presence of the Spirit of God in them, a Spirit who is suggesting to them their full and true identity, their real value as human beings, and the job they have to do in the world. The voice of the minister must awaken what is truly human in man, so that men will begin to respect themselves. From this all else will follow.

7

THE OTHER WORLD

One of the characteristics of the peak religious experience, as we have said, is that it is numinous. It is freighted with a sense of other-worldly reality. One of the chief functions of theology in the past was to give people some kind of description of this other world. If life after death is the goal of the religious life on earth, naturally people were curious about it. They wanted to know if it would be worth the price they would have to pay for it.

The symbol of the great banquet prepared by the king may have only a messianic and not an overtly eschatological tone as it is rendered by Luke (14:15-24), but in the parallel pericope in Matthew (22:1-14) according to the opinion of some scholars reference is made to the future life. The phrase "weeping and gnashing of teeth" (v. 13) has for Matthew definite eschatological overtones. Further evidence of the understanding by the early Christians of these texts as references to a celestial banquet is given by catacumbal art.

If it can be presumed that everybody likes a party, and if among oriental peoples it was considered a special breach of etiquette to decline an invitation to a feast given by a prominent person, the parable might well imply an indictment against the servants of the king. The failure of the prophets and ministers of the Lord to show forth what he had promised to those who serve him faithfully and loyally as something thoroughly pleasant and delightful prompted Jesus to emphasize this aspect of his mission. But even his doctrine was at first rejected, and he was put to death because of it, since it seemed far different from what the prophets had foretold. Only eventually, after Jesus' resurrection, could the idea he proposed about man's future life, about eternal feasting or misery, be accepted.

Up until very recently theology has been very parsimonious in its speculations on the life of the world to come. The old models and images were considered sacrosanct, and consequently they failed to be demythologized so that they could be integrated with rapidly developing scientific views of the universe. The first Russian cosmonaut undoubtedly thought he was, as a good atheist and loyal party member, shaking the faith of many when he announced that he found no evidence of God in the space above the earth. Because theology failed to do its job, ministers were unable properly to do theirs. They could not tell their people where God's heaven was, nor just what it might be like. They had to let the faithful think that it was a big banquet hall located somewhere up above the earth.

Anthropology gives evidence of a deep acculturation of concepts about the particulars of the life after death promised by most of the world's religions. Among the most affluent peoples it is seen essentially as a translation of earthly life to a different and better locale. Among the extremely poor it entails a total and perfect reversal of earthly experience. Many peoples, particularly in the east, hope to survive by means of some kind of metempsychosis; they believe that they will continue to live on earth, but in a different form, in other human bodies or those of animals. Still others hope to achieve a state of altered existence, to live in some analogous sense as shades or ghosts. In pantheistic beliefs death means reabsorption into more formally divine modalities of existence. Still other peoples believe in survival only of the community; individuals will pass away and become part of some cosmic consciousness.

Almost every religion writes its own ticket to the future life, a ticket that meets the needs and propensities of the culture it serves. For some the only requirement is a proper burial, like mummification, or a bodily sign, like a pierced nose or ear lobes. Others demand some kind of ritualistic initiation to the religious body. A special kind of knowledge or gnosis or the observance of certain taboos or ethical norms are the most important factors for still others. Some religions demand all of these signs or certain combinations of them. But the people find out definitely from their priests or shamans just what they must do, and what they have to hope for if they do fulfill the requirements.

In our time Karl Rahner has made some attempt to address himself to one of the difficulties posed by the Christian concept of the other world. Thomistic theologians maintain that the human soul to the extent that it differs from a pure spirit like an angel must always retain some essential relationship to matter. The body and soul make up the complete substance of man. The soul existing without the body is not really a complete substance; nor, consequently, can the soul alone really be considered a human person: it is only a supposite. To continue to be what it is after death, then, the soul must remain in a transcendental relationship to some material reality.

Rahner is of the opinion that this relationship has to be real, that is, that there has to be some definite material substance toward which the soul is essentially orientated; it does not suffice merely to have a tendency in the soul toward matter in general. He would not think that this definite material reality is precisely the dead body for it ceases to be a *unum per se* without its proper form; nor could it be the individual molecules or atoms that make up the dead body. Rather it would seem that the soul, freed from its relationship with this definite segment of matter, is now able to assume a much fuller and more extensive kind of relationship. Because it is still a soul and not a pure spirit, it cannot exist in some kind of "acosmic" state. What it achieves through death is a pancosmic relationship, that is, it is now transcendentally orientated toward the whole universe. This does not mean, of course, that in some way the whole universe becomes the soul's body, or that the soul becomes universally present wherever there is any matter. Rahner explains the relationship of the soul to universal matter in existentialistic terms as a basic openness to the whole universe. As form, the soul's influence was restricted directly to its body; but after death this limitation is removed. The soul can roam through the universe and exercise its influence, not as a form, but as an efficient cause, on matter wherever it might be found. This action in the universe defines and preserves its essential orientation toward matter.

Some of the Fathers of the Church, notably among them St. Gregory the Great and St. Jerome, at times advance the idea that in eschatological times heaven and earth will not completely pass away, will not be totally destroyed. They will rather pass over into a new form of existence. There will not be a different heaven and a different earth; the present ones will be transformed into a dwelling place for the elect when they receive their bodies again at the general resurrection.

Theological speculations like those of Rahner (and Boros, who seems to have an idea very much like his) and some of the Fathers may open the way to a consideration of the other world as not so distinct and different from this one. And if such a consideration is possible, certain scientific facts may well exercise an influence upon the theological development of a model of the other world for the people of our time.

Karl Marx once said that man is his action upon the world. Indeed, if we consider the physical makeup of the human body we find it a seething mass of electro-chemical forces in action and reaction, never at any one given time exactly the same as it was before or is to be after. There is no scientific instrument at present sensitive enough to measure at some distance from the human body the electric fields or electromagnetic waves set up by this action. Yet they do exist, though the energy output is extremely small. The power generated by the human brain for a whole hour is just about enough to light up a small light bulb. But small as it is, there is no reason to believe that this energy, or at least the electromagnetic component of it, does not follow the physical laws of propagation. The potential of electromagnetic energy will vary linearly in inverse proportion to the square of the distance from the radiating source. When one has an infinitesmally small amount to begin with, one would have hardly anything left at a distance from the earth, say, equivalent to that of the moon. But the point is that, irretrievable as it might be with the known possibilities of instrumentation, it is never absolutely lost. As the distance increases the potential difference to ground approaches zero. But, theoretically speaking, it never reaches zero. Given the proper detector, it might even be discovered billions of light years later at the outer reaches of the currently known universe. If I could travel at a speed many times greater than that of light and station myself in space at the proper distance from earth with a highly efficient and extremely sensitive photomultiplier device, it would theoretically be possible for me to get a view of earth as it was in the past, for instance, in 1775. And if I could pan in without distortion on a particular segment of the total maelstrom of radiation, I might possibly get a picture of George Washington in action. It sounds like science-fiction, and indeed, writers and television script-men have capitalized on this notion, but it is not without foundation in scientific fact.

In the light of these data, Rahner's view may not be as farfetched as it might seem to the practical man of today. It may well be a theological vision that can be coordinated in some way with the scientific knowledge of the present.

More important for our discussion of the other world with relation to religious experience in this one, however, is the current scientific view of the space-time continuum in which man is enveloped. Tridimensional space and time are the four parameters in which human earthly experience is unfolded and along which it is measured to the extent that it can be. Yet these parameters are, as is well known both from philosophy and science, logical constructs corresponding not fully, but only in some basic way to the relational realities they represent. The basis of that correspondence is in the subjective percepts of duration, of binocular visual fields and tactile contact with the energy vectors of matter. But we may well believe that the as yet hypothetical creature from Mars with radically different sense organs and a differently functioning brain would be able to perceive other dimensions of reality.

There is some suggestion of the variability of dimensional perception in the movie 2001: *A Space Odyssey*. At the end of the picture one of the travellers on the spaceship Discovery I, having now aged many decades finds himself rather suddenly in an apartment furnished in the style of Louis XIV. Its ceiling and floor are translucent. He sees himself in a mirror and beholds there a body even more advanced in age seated at a small table on which is spread an elegant meal. A wine glass falls and shatters, and he sees himself on his death bed looking at the monolith that has signified a numinous presence beckoning always a transcendence of past consciousness throughout the picture; every time it appears consciousness is expanded to encounter a new dimension of reality. On the astronaut's head is a translucent orb shaped like a space-helmet. It expands, and he finds himself in it like a child tucked away in a celestial womb.

The relative nature of the measuring sticks of time is well illustrated by the physical phenomenon known as the Doppler effect. If I am sitting in my car at a railroad crossing waiting for a train to go by its whistle sounds more shrill to me as the train approaches and more low-pitched as it recedes. But a person on the train perceives it to have the same pitch all the time. As the train approaches the crossing more sound waves strike my ear per unit of time than strike the ear of a person on the train, since the speed of the train has to be added to the equation when it takes into account my position. Just the opposite occurs as the train moves away from me. Its speed has to be subtracted in the equation I would use to get the number of waves striking my fixed spot per unit of time. This phenomenon applies to all kinds of radiation, including light (which is our measuring stick for time) as Einstein well real-ized. The shift toward red in the spectrograph of stars photo-graphed in their position far from the earth indicates their motion to be away from the earth; were they moving toward us the shift would occur in the violet end of the visible spec-trum. From this evidence the scientific theory of the expanding universe originates.

It also follows that on a spaceship moving at speeds ap-proaching that of light away from the earth time would pass more slowly relative to the earth. Thus while the astronauts spend one year according to their calculations aboard ship, earth calendars might advance five. Of course, in coming back the process would be reversed, so that when they landed their time would jibe exactly with earth's. Relative to an entirely different time system, say, that of Mars, ahead of the space-ship as it moves away from earth, time would speed up. Thus on the same spaceship time would be slowing down and speed-ing up at the same time, but relative to two different systems.

Nor are spatial dimensions any less relative, though it may be harder to see. Length, width and depth are all mental constructs based on perception. No natural reality exactly corresponds to them. I perceive now the edge of my desk as a straight line. I know that no such thing as a line exists, but the edge of the desk is very real to me and seems to represent one dimension of the total structure. An adventure into the micro-cosm would soon change my mind. If I could see the molecules and atoms arranged along what I perceived to be the edge of my desk, I would be in a new world of dimension. The edge really is indefinable. Brownian movements send desk material (if I could identify it) into air material and vice versa. The adjacent wall too is involved in the transfer. No wonder Einstein could say that, given enough time, I might be able to perceive the desk pass through the wall and into the next room.

Einstein rather simply illustrates both the relational and interlocking nature of our perceptual universe of space-time.

It constitutes a unit system in which all dimensions are both relative to one another and connected with one another. Suppose, he says, we take our instruments for measuring space and time onto a platform which we believe to be suspended motionless in space. We will never be able to prove, of course, that our platform is really motionless, even if we can sight other objects in space, because even though we do not seem to move relative to them, the whole system may actually be moving. We do tend, however, to designate the place where we are as motionless in such a situation, and ascribe any movement we perceive to other bodies. Suppose there is another platform identical in shape with ours moving by us at a speed of about 5×10^8 feet per second. Granted that we could get a glimpse of this platform as it sped by, and that we knew we had painted a perfect circle on it, what would we see? Not a circle at all, but an ellipse. And we would note that its short diameter would lie in the direction of the motion. The amount of its shortening from the full diameter of the circle we had painted would vary in direct proportion to the speed of the platform, so that, if the second platform accelerated to the speed of light and we could still observe it, what we had perceived as a circle we would now see as a straight line perpendicular to the direction of motion. A dimension would have been lost! An observer on the moving platform would, of course, still see the circle as a circle. But he too, and any measuring instrument he had with him on the moving platform would lose a spatial dimension relative to the supposedly fixed platform. If we slowed the moving platform to produce an ellipse relative to the stationary one and placed in the short diameter a yardstick which we used to measure the exact diameter of the circle we drew, it, of course, would still indicate one yard, for its dimension would be reduced also along the line of travel. At slower speeds, to be sure, this shortening would be imperceptible.

This is not scientific fiction, but the stuff out of which the scientifically recognized theory of relativity grew. And it is based upon unassailable geometric and mathematical reasoning. In the tridimensional, ordinary, visible world of Euclid, the world of the layman in mathematics and physics there is no accounting for this phenomenal chimera. But in our time the terminator of consciousness has been pushed back, our consciousness has been expanded, to envision the reality of this quadridimensional understanding of the universe. In today's world, the quadridimensional world of atomic physics and astrophysics, the Euclidian chimera becomes a fact. The geometry of Euclid supposes a world of three dimensions. The geometry of Riemann is open to a world of n-dimensions. In this very real world of ours there are possibilities of an indefinite number of dimensional systems, each one self-contained, but able to relate the same reality in different and even contrary ways, system to system.

Because of the quality of our consciousness now, we live in a quadridimensional world, a world of time, length, width and depth (tlwd), for short, the world of time. The other world to which we believe the departed go, and in which God dwells in a vastly different way from the way he appears in this one, has only one known dimension: eternity (e) but may well have others also that will turn up in some future theological investigation (xyz). We may conceive the two worlds, then, as two diverse dimensional systems (tlwd - exyz) of the same vast material reality we call the universe. There is no contradiction at all if relative to the diverse systems of time and eternity radically different things happen, from our perspective, "at the same time." Thus while we are placing the body of a deceased person in the grave in the dimensional system by which our consciousness is now bounded, the tlwd system, relative to the totally different system of our belief, the exyz system, that body is risen and taking part in celestial activity. The terminator of consciousness of that person is moved to allow the perception of this entirely new dimensional system.

The reality that we call the universe may indeed fold in

upon itself and well up outside of itself to form the foundation of any number of dimensional systems. The only symbols that we have to represent these possible systems are mathematical, because all our words are the product of our customary percepts of dimension. How can we speak except in terms of length, width and depth? But the mathematicians and physicists assure us not only that in their language there is absolutely no contradiction or absurdity in such an hypothesis, but that certain physical data, like the deviation of photons in gravitational fields, could be better explained by such a theory.

If a scientific hypothesis like this can find its way into our theology as a model for the other world that is more intelligible to modern man, then God may not be as far off as one might suspect. Peak religious experience might involve only a repositioning of the terminator of consciousness to provide a fleeting glimpse of the other system. It would be a moment of *kairos*, when one becomes conscious in some nebulous way of eternity touching time. And if such moments could be better cultivated and appreciated, the quality of Christian consciousness itself might well be altered and expanded to allow a better view of this other dimensional system.

In the Middle Ages in highly Christian cultures superstitious belief placed certain spaces and certain times outside of the ambit of this world. Churches could become places of refuge for criminals of all kinds, even murderers. Architectural design, light streaming through stained-glass windows as well as the mystic rites and symbols its walls enclosed created the impression among the people that the space a church occupied was truly sacral, a little bit of heaven upon earth, not a part of this world at all. The hymns they sang then reflected the same notion:

> Alto ex Olympi vertice
> Summi Parentis Filius,
> Ceu monte desectus lapis

Terras in imas decidens,
Domus supernae et infimae
Utrumque iunxit angulum.

Indeed many of the faithful felt that the time they spent at Mass or in other liturgical worship would not be counted by God in the span of their earthly life. They could actually live longer by spending as much time as possible at sacred rites. Such ideas adumbrate in a primitive and undeveloped way the compenetration of worlds which today's consciousness can well embrace and purge of superstitious elements.

Experience at times of the other world lying across the terminator of consciousness is a very potent factor in leading men even in today's sophisticated society to wonder and perhaps to affirm with Pierre Teilhard de Chardin that something significant is afoot in the universe. That significant thing can well be seen as a love that is unlimited and surpasses man's wildest imaginings. It is pushing, impelling, guiding and directing the scattered elements of the universe to seek one another, so that not only this world but also the next may come into being.

BIBLIOGRAPHY

Books

Alexander, A. **Thoughts on Religious Experience**. London, Banner of Truth Trust, 1968.

Baruzi, J. **Création religieuse et pensée contemplative**. Paris Aubier, 1951.

Bouquet, A. **Religious Experience; its Nature, Types and Validity**. Cambridge, Heffer, 1968.

Damboriena, P. **Tongues as of Fire: Pentecostalism in Contemporary Christianity**. N.Y., Corpus Books, 1969.

Dedek, J. **Experimental Knowledge of the Indwelling Trinity: an Historical Study of the Doctrine of St. Thomas**. Mundelein, Ill., St. Mary of the Lake Seminary, 1958.

Eliade, M. **Mephistopheles and the Androgyne: Studies in Religious Myth and Symbol**. N.Y., Sheed & Ward, 1965.

Freud, S. **On Creativity and the Unconscious**. N.Y., Harper, 1958. **Psychopathology of Everyday Life**. N.Y., New American Library, 1951.

Fromm, E. **Psychoanalysis and Religion**. N.Y., Bantam Books, 1967.

Galtier, P. **L'habitation en nous des Trois Personnes**. Rome, Université gregorienne, 1949.

Gardeil, A. **La structure de l'âme et l'expérience mystique**. Paris, Gabalda, 1927.

Garrigou-Lagrange, R. **Le sens du mystère et le clair-obscure intellectuel**. Paris, Desclée, 1934.

Godin, A. **From Religious Experience to Religious Attitude**. Chicago, Loyola University Press, 1965.

Goldbrunner, J. **Cure of Mind and Cure of Soul: Depth Psychology and Pastoral Care**. Notre Dame, Ind., University of Notre Dame, 1962.

Homans, P., ed. **The Dialogue between Theology and Psychology**. Chicago, University of Chicago Press, 1968.

James, W. **The Varieties of Religious Experience**. N.Y., Longmans, 1952.

John of the Cross, St. **Ascent of Mount Carmel**. Garden City, N.Y., Doubleday, 1958.

Dark Night of the Soul. Garden City, N.Y., Doubleday, 1959.

Spiritual Canticle. Garden City, N.Y., Doubleday, 1961.

Johnston, W. **The Still Point; Reflections on Zen and Christian Mysticism.** N.Y., Fordham University Press, 1970.

Lepp, I. **The Depths of the Soul; a Christian Approach to Psychoanalysis.** N.Y., Doubleday, 1967.

Mawson, S. **The Validity of Religious Experience.** London, Inter-Varsity Fellowship, 1965.

May, R., ed. **Symbolism in Religion and Literature.** N.Y., G. Braziller, 1960.

Meissner, W., ed. **Foundations for a Psychology of Grace.** Glen Rock, N.J., Paulist Press, 1966.

Miller, D. **Gods and Games; toward a Theology of Play.** N.Y., World Publishing Co., 1970.

Mouroux, J. **The Christian Experience.** N.Y., Sheed & Ward, 1954.

Nédoncelle, M. **Vers une philosophie de l'amour et de la personne.** Paris, Aubier, 1957.

Nos sens et Dieu. Bruges, Desclée, De Brouwer, 1954.

O'Brien, M. & Steimel, R., eds. **Psychological Aspects of Spiritual Development.** Washington, D.C., Catholic University of America Press, 1964.

O'Doherty, E. **Religion and Personality Problems.** Staten Island, N.Y. Alba House, 1964.

Otto, R. **The Idea of the Holy.** London, Penguin Books, 1959.

Poulain, A. **The Graces of Interior Prayer.** London, Routledge & Kegan Paul, 1950.

Il problema dell'esperienza religiosa. Brescia, Morcelliana, 1961.

Rabut, O. **L'expérience religieuse fondamentale.** Paris, Casterman, 1969.

Rawcliffe, D. **Illusions and Delusions of the Supernatural and the Occult.** N.Y., Dover, 1959.

Smart, N. **The Religious Experience of Mankind.** N.Y., Scribners, 1969.

Suzuki, D. **Zen Buddhism.** Garden City, N.Y., Doubleday, 1956.

Thurston, H. **The Physical Phenomena of Mysticism.** London, Burns & Oates, 1952.

Watkin, E. **The Bow in the Clouds; an Essay towards the Integration of Experience.** N.Y., Macmillan, 1932.

White, V. **God and the Unconscious.** Chicago, Regnery, 1953.

Articles

Baron, R. "Reason and History; Experience and the Mystery of Salvation in Religious Pedagogy," **Lumen Vitae 10:489.**

Baudouin, C. "Expérience du yoga et christianisme," **Vie spirituelle supplement** 43:486.

Bortolaso, G. "Filosofia ed esperienza religiosa," **Civiltà cattolica** 112:53.

Bozzo, E. "Theology and Religious Experience," **Theological Studies** 31:415.

Caster, M. van. "Towards a Christian Understanding of Experience," **Lumen Vitae 25:599.**

Colborn, F. "The Theology of Grace: Present Trends and Future Directions," **Theological Studies** 31:692.

Cousins, E. "Models and the Future of Theology," **Continuum** 7:78.

Cox, H. "Secular Search for Religious Experience," **Theology Today** 25:320.

Deprit, A. "Death as Experience of the Creative Presence of God," **Downside Review** 74:329.

Guardini, R. "Phenomenology of Religious Experience," **Philosophy Today** 6:88.

Guitton, J. "Psychology of Religious Experience," **Philosophy Today** 6:93.

Holstein, H. "L'expérience chrétienne," **Études** 277:239.

Johann, R. "Nearness of God," **America** 108:21.

Kitagawa, J. "Human Situations and Religious Experience," **Criterion** 3:32.

Letter, P. de. "Encounter with God," **Thought** 36:5.

Lonergan, B. "Religious Experience and Theological Method," **Theology Digest** 7:34.

Lotz, J. "Metaphysical and Religious Experience," **Philosophy Today** 2:240.

"Philosophy of Religious Experience," **Philosophy Today** 6:97.

McDonnell, K. "I Believe that I Might Experience," **Continuum 5:673.**

Mounier, E. "That Worst, Most Dangerous Life," **Cross Currents** 11:25.

Nachtergaele, J. "Scientific Method and Spiritual Experience," **Lumen Vitae** 13:650.

Payne, J. "William James and Religion," **Dominicana** 45:336.

"Religion and Parapsychology," **Pastoral Psychology** 21:5.

Schoonenberg, P. "Revelation and Experience," **Lumen Vitae** 25:551.

Sloyan, G. "Experience of Mystery; Requisite for Theology," **Catholic Educational Review** 55:289.

Smith, J. "In What Sense Can We Speak of Experiencing God?" **Journal of Religion** 50:229.

Watkin, E. "Repose of the Abyss," **Spiritual Life** 2:156.

Weigel, G. "The Protestant Principle: the Encounter of God," **Catholic World** 192:28.

Widmer G. "An Essay in Protestant Philosophy," **Philosophy Today** 6:93.

Yurrita, J. "La reconciliacion como experiencia religiosa," **Razon y fe,** 164:49.

INDEX